*Katie,*
*Here's to.*

# Raising the Bar:

## Legendary Rainmakers Share Their
## Business Development Secrets

*Robin Hensley*

# Raising the Bar:

## Legendary Rainmakers Share Their Business Development Secrets

By Robin M. Hensley

*Individual Coaching for Business Development*

Schroder Media

Published by Schroder Media, LLC
1355 Peachtree Street, NE, Suite 1250
Atlanta, GA 30309
www.schroderpr.com

Publisher: Chris Schroder
Editorial Director: Jan Butsch Schroder
Cover and book design: Heidi Rizzi
Copy editing: Blane Bachelor, Beverly Molander, Carole Ashkinaze
Videographer and photographer: Reid Childers
Videographer's assistant: Evelyn Anne Johnston


ISBN: 978-0-9762288-3-7
Printed and bound in Korea
First printing, 2009
Schroder Media

To my Mom, for always believing in me,
and whose never-ending strength
is my constant inspiration.

"Start early and begin
raising the bar throughout the day."
— *Bruce Jenner*
*American track athlete, author, speaker*

"It is never too late to be
what you might have been."
— *George Eliot,*
*English novelist, whose real name was Mary Ann Evans*

Atlanta Legal Aid Society

Robin M. Hensley is proud to donate a majority of the profits of *Raising the Bar: Legendary Rainmakers Share Their Business Development Secrets* to benefit the Endowment Fund of the Atlanta Legal Aid Society. Ms. Hensley has been on the advisory board of Atlanta Legal Aid since 2003.

Atlanta Legal Aid Society is the primary provider of civil legal services to low-income people in Fulton, DeKalb, Gwinnett, Clayton, and Cobb counties. Lawyers handle more than 20,000 cases a year, primarily involving housing, family, and senior citizen issues. Begun in 1924 by seventeen prominent local attorneys, Atlanta Legal Aid has meant access to justice for countless individuals.

For more information or to learn how you can help, please visit www.atlantalegalaid.org.

# Table of Contents

# Introduction

*Everybody is always marketing. But most lawyers have no idea how to sell anything. They don't teach salesmanship in law school.*
*– Judge Griffin Bell*

If I had to sum up why I do what I do, I'd turn to these words from Judge Griffin Bell. As a business development coach, I work with many lawyers on client development, precisely because they have not been taught how to, yet they are expected to do so to succeed in their careers.

It was during my coaching work with a law firm in Alabama that I first had the idea for this book. I was working with Jack Miller, who hired me to coach the attorneys in his firm, Miller Hamilton Snider & Odum. (This firm recently combined with Jones Walker.)

While I worked with Mr. Miller's firm, I was able to spend a lot of time with him. He shared with me the way he founded the firm, how he built up his client base and his philosophy on leadership and client development. I was fascinated by his stories and the wisdom he shared.

When I met him, Mr. Miller was battling cancer. He has now survived a second bout of cancer and is in remission. It occurred to me that if his stories were not preserved, we'd be in danger of losing the benefits of that wisdom.

Around this time, I was sitting at an Atlanta Legal Aid Society board meeting, pondering how I could make an additional contribution to this worthy organization, other than just by writing a check. I thought about a business associate, Bob Littell, who had co-authored a book called *Power NetWeaving*. He was donating the royalties from that book to Junior Achievement.

So the idea hit me – I would write a book to memorialize the great leaders of the legal community. I could preserve their seasoned advice so that others could be inspired by their actions and their wisdom. And a majority of the profits would go to benefit Atlanta Legal Aid's endowment fund.

So how to select the people to profile? I asked many attorneys, judges, and other leaders in Atlanta and Georgia who they thought were the best of the best. We came up with a list of ten people. I am so thankful to all ten of these people who gave so generously of their time and wisdom for this book.

It has been my great privilege to visit with them over the past six months and hear their tales of success, but also learn about the struggles that they faced during their careers. I strolled through the beautiful gardens at Paul Webb's cabin in Helen, Georgia, ate fudge cake with Bobby Lee Cook at his favorite diner in Summerville, peeked at Clay Long's balcony to see the nests of the peregrine falcons that roost there every year, and sat spellbound with former Governor Carl Sanders as he expounded on decades of Atlanta history. Emmet Bondurant shared his story of how he ended up arguing a case before the U.S. Supreme Court when he was just twenty-six years of age.

Miles Alexander entertained me with stories of product liability cases, Chilton Varner intrigued me with her assertion that being a trial lawyer is like playing a three-dimensional chess game,

Frank Love told me about playing a round of golf with Mickey Rooney, and Richard Sinkfield shared with us an important lesson he learned accidentally as an associate barely out of law school that he passes down to younger attorneys.

Although I was unable to meet with Judge Bell in person, I was able to correspond with him about his contribution and am so very pleased and honored that he was willing to share from his decades of experience.

We videotaped the rest of these interviews, and excerpts of each one are found in the accompanying DVD included in the back of the book. It was especially important to me to preserve their words of wisdom in their own voices, and in some cases to preserve the lovely Southern accent you don't hear too much anymore.

It's true that times are very different now from the days when most started their careers. Although they worked very long hours, there were no "billable hours" back then; you just did the job until it was done. And of course there were no cell phones, fax machines, computers or even voicemail to facilitate communication. But attorneys back then found their own ways. Judge Bell talks about his early days in Savannah when all the lawyers would gather at a local saloon every day at eleven in the morning to discuss and settle cases.

In the days before specialization, many of these attorneys started out handling murder cases, divorces and adoptions – whatever kinds of cases they were handed. And of course, compensation has changed a bit: When Paul Webb first moved to Atlanta and interviewed for jobs, the going rate for a lawyer was $100 a month.

Although many things have changed, there is still so much wisdom to be gleaned from the older members of the bar, and so many of their truths are just as applicable today as they were many years ago.

As you may expect, many of the ten lawyers had several things in common. Several of them had attended law school at Harvard, and many had served courageously in World War II. More than a few got involved in politics; we have a former governor and a U.S. attorney general in the group. There were several from small towns such as Lyerly, Georgia and Demopolis, Alabama. There were a few who had considered other careers – college professor or minister – when they were young. And of course, many were involved with the Atlanta Legal Aid Society, with Emmet Bondurant and Paul Webb serving terms as president.

But one thing they all shared was a dedication to and a passion for the law. Many expressed the feeling that it is a privilege to be a lawyer. "There is not a day goes by that I don't look in the mirror and thank God I'm a lawyer," said Mr. Webb.

It is with a sense of great privilege that I present you with their stories in my book, *Raising the Bar: Legendary Rainmakers Share Their Business Development Secrets.*

This book is for attorneys and any others who are inspired by the stories of actual people and their lives, and what made them successful. After listening to all of these people and the lessons they impart, I believe that anyone in professional service careers can learn from these great leaders who have accomplished so much.

I hope that you enjoy reading their stories and hearing highlights of their interviews (on the accompanying DVD), and feel the same sense of inspiration and admiration as I did.


– *Robin M. Hensley*

# Lawyers

# Miles Alexander

Partner and Co-Chairman
Kilpatrick Stockton

An intellectual property lawyer, Miles Alexander attributes his success to mentors at his firm and their legendary predecessors whose representation dates back to the origins of The Coca-Cola Company. In the same breath as he pays homage to his mentors, he attributes his and his firm's preeminence in the intellectual property field to their ability to recruit outstanding young lawyers who develop different skills and share common goals.

The beneficiaries of those efforts over the years have included clients with such esteemed intellectual property and brands as PepsiCo, General Mills, the Walt Disney Company, the General Electric Company, Frito-Lay, A&P, Harley-Davidson, Dominos Pizza, Rolls-Royce, and the Estate of Martin Luther King, Jr., Inc., to name just a few.

Among Mr. Alexander's achievements are protection of the "I Have a Dream" speech, the establishment of Fritos as a trademark and not a generic term for corn chips, and the protection of Rolls-Royce's distinctive Flying Lady, RR and grill designs against imitation. He has also protected and defended the famous marks of Superman, Wonder Woman, Betty Crocker, Dominos, The Monkees, Red Cross, Adidas, Reebok, the Blue Cross and Blue Shield Association, Lay's, Doritos, R.E.M., Imax, Big Star, Kix, Wheaties, Cingular, BellSouth, Jell-O, and myriad Fortune 500 companies in more than fifty years as a lawyer to whom many clients have looked when their most valuable assets, their brand and identity, were at stake.

An elder statesman not only of the Georgia, but also of the U.S. and the international intellectual property (IP) bars, Mr. Alexander has an office filled with mementos from grateful clients, reflecting cases in which he has been involved. These include a plaque from the rock band R.E.M., needlepoint pillows with images of Adidas shoes, and a hand-made Cabbage Patch Kid in a pinstripe lawyer's suit with a briefcase. The latter commemorates an enormous recovery he and a collaborating attorney won from the Topps Garbage Pail Kids for dilution of the Cabbage Patch Kids brand.

There are also Harley Barbie dolls and a "Tushie Roll" roll of toilet paper in Tootsie Roll colors, together with other collectors' items, crystalline glass awards and sculptures from a lifetime of contributions to the legal profession and to the community.

Why are trademarks so important? "It's all about protecting the brand, which is often a client's most valuable asset," Mr. Alexander said. For example, "If every Coca-Cola plant was destroyed by a catastrophe, eliminating all of the company's tangible assets, it could still borrow one billion dollars with just the Coca-Cola trademark as security. The brand gives you the value. Most companies don't have anything tangible approximating the value of their brand."

*Miles Alexander at basic training. "I made more in the military than I did in law practice."*

An honors graduate of both Emory University and Harvard Law School, Mr. Alexander attended high school in Virginia, Japan, New York, and Florida, moving around the world with his mother and his stepfather, a career military man, while spending summers and vacations with his father in Montreal. He worked as a summer associate at the predecessor firm of Kilpatrick Stockton in 1954 and 1955. After serving two years as a United States Air Force Judge Advocate, he returned to Harvard Law School as a teaching fellow, responsible for courses in trial practice and legal writing. "I actually had Michael Dukakis and Justice Scalia as first-year students," he said. He remembered grading Justice Scalia's practice exam papers, stating: "I gave him straight A's, despite our philosophical differences."

Mr. Alexander might have remained in education, but his wife, Elaine, also a teacher, was ready to settle down in one place and have children, so they returned to Atlanta. Mr. Alexander rejoined Kilpatrick, Cody, Rogers, McClatchey & Regenstein, Kilpatrick Stockton's predecessor, in 1958. When he joined the firm, there were fourteen lawyers, making it the largest firm in Atlanta. "We were called 'We the People' because we were a 'double-digit' law firm."

At that time, many Atlanta firms did not hire African Americans, women, or Jews. Fortunately for Mr. Alexander, who is Jewish, and for Kilpatrick Stockton, it was one of the major firms open to him. "I think my firm did so in part because one of the founding members, Harold Hirsch, was Jewish and all the non-Jewish senior partners were his protégés who revered him," Mr. Alexander said.

But starting his legal career involved a pay cut. "I made more in the military than I did in law practice. The salaries in New York law firms when I started were $4,800 a year and Atlanta was generally at $3,600 a year, with our firm at $4,200. Compensation did go up rather rapidly after that. However, young people were not drawn to the law for money at that time. You could make more by teaching at law school, where my salary had been almost twice that available from any law firm."

Mr. Alexander described his practice then as eclectic. "We had seven partners and

*Harvard Law School Faculty–October 1957*
*Miles Alexander is pictured in the third row from the top, fifth from the right.*

seven associates, all of whom always had assignments from all seven partners. So I could be working on a patent infringement case for Mead Corporation one day; defending a slip-and-fall case for Colonial Stores Supermarket the next; then a tax case, corporate merger, or public offering for Frito-Lay; a government contract for Lockheed; a Swift & Co. strike; and an executive's divorce case, all while drawing up wills and trusts for officers of the Fulton National Bank (later Bank South and Bank of America). We were all required to litigate on the theory that you could not counsel clients in evaluating a dispute unless you had personally handled litigation. We did all the work for a leading insurance carrier to make sure young associates had an opportunity to appear frequently in court early in their careers."

One thing Mr. Alexander wasn't expected to do was bring in clients. "The firm was very successful in terms of having a stable of loyal clients, so when we came with the firm as young associates, partners weren't really interested in our bringing clients or business into the firm," he said. In fact, he often did work for good friends without charging them legal fees they could ill afford as young architects, doctors, or businessmen. Many of these contemporaries later developed into large clients who remained loyal, among them Cooper Carry, Inc., a leading international architectural firm.

The firm also represented many large corporations from their early days as start-ups such as Scientific Atlanta, H.W. Lay, and Aaron Rents. Some of these could not afford counsel at the beginning, so the firm did their legal work without charge or in exchange for stock as they grew. "Sometimes we were betting that these companies would become successful because they were good business people," Alexander said. "Sometimes it was out of friendship because these were people you were close to socially, and they needed assistance and you had the talent or skills to provide it.

"In the early years, the compensation paid to young lawyers was so low that there was no need for concern about billable hours or keeping track of time. You just worked on something until you got it right. People didn't care how long it took as long as the work was of the highest quality. Our firm's retainers covered the overhead and retainers were reviewed at the end of the year to determine if an additional fee in excess of retainer was appropriate."

Kilpatrick Stockton was able to attract large national clients who were looking for counsel in Atlanta because of its reputation as counsel to The Coca-Cola Company since the late nineteenth and early twentieth century. "That was particularly true in the intellectual property area because other large firms in Atlanta did not have a trademark, patent or copyright practice, which resided primarily in small boutique law practices for most of the twentieth century," Mr. Alexander recalled. In addition, Atlanta became the leading city in the South and courts in Atlanta were viewed, correctly or incorrectly, as more likely to protect intellectual property rights. Atlanta was a rail and later an airline hub city, making travel to it easier."

Kilpatrick Stockton now has an international reputation for its intellectual property practice, with more than 120 dedicated IP attorneys, and support from its even larger litigation group.

*A firm portrait of the senior partners who began with the firm in the fifties, then known as Kilpatrick, Cody, Rogers, McClatchey & Regenstein; (l-r) Tom Shelton, Miles Alexander, Hal Abrams, Barry Phillips, George Haley.*

One of the firm's early successes in branding, while protecting the Coca-Cola mark throughout the world, was the Coca-Cola bottle. Uniform packaging back in the early 1900s was not common in the soft drink industry, with separately owned bottlers, and Coca-Cola beverages were sold in a variety of bottles, depending on the territory in which the bottling company was located. Harold Hirsh, senior partner of the law firm while also serving as General Counsel of The Coca-Cola Company, suggested that the company create uniform bottles to make imitation difficult and reinforce its brand.

"He hired a renowned glassblower and talked various bottlers into having uniform bottles. This distinctive bottle became a world-famous trademark, probably one of the first configuration trademarks of its kind," Mr. Alexander said.

Similarly, Ernest Rogers, who was mentored by Harold Hirsch, recognized that "Coke," although not registered as a mark, became one through repeated consumer requests for a "Coke." After long resistance from the company, because of its perceived early negative association with cocaine, Mr. Rogers became a moving force in embracing and building "Coke" into a world-famous mark.

But Mr. Alexander said that Mr. Rogers could have been the end of the line of intellectual property lawyers for his firm. "One of my great mentors was the great Renaissance lawyer, Ernest 'Jelly' Rogers. From the thirties to the early fifties, he was the lawyer doing virtually all of the firm's IP work and, by the time I arrived, he indicated that unless some young lawyer in our firm found it interesting and wanted to become involved in it, he was going to refer IP work to Washington DC where there were a number of firms specializing in this area of the law. He had involved me in antitrust work where dominant trademarks were often a factor in government challenges to mergers and price discrimination. He also had me working on a Givenchy perfume case to stop exporters in Europe from sending Givenchy perfume to the U.S. and rebottling it. Our client was Genesco, which owned the trademark in the United States and had expended a great deal of money and energy in advertising it. We were attempting to stop the unauthorized importation of this product through customs. We were successful and Genesco was able to halt the objectionable activity. Mr. Rogers sent copies of my research to a number of clients, promoting me as the firm's new outstanding IP lawyer, with accolades that would make me his loyal devotee for life."

Thus, Miles Alexander as a very young lawyer became the heir to a continuing great trademark practice.

"I began to specialize in that area in the late fifties. One of my first cases was for General Mills, a long-time firm client. I had to go down to Tampa, Florida and file suit against the Betty Crocker Paint Company. That was a time when if the infringing product did not have the same descriptive qualities as the original (for example paint was not a bakery product), the law did not prevent it from being sold under the same Betty Crocker mark," Mr. Alexander recalled. But the judge was so offended by the defendant trading on the famous Betty Crocker name for a paint company that he enjoined them even though there was no legal authority to do so. It was more than thirty years later before federal dilution laws protected famous marks against use of unrelated goods or services."

Although he handled patent litigation in the late fifties, Mr. Alexander observed that he would certainly not try a patent case that early in his career if he were starting out now. "It is a much more specialized field today and attracts lawyers who have a sophisticated background with advance degrees in chemistry, engineering, and other areas," he said. "I have a hard time screwing in a light bulb."

In a major case in the early sixties, his firm represented Frito-Lay. The Fritos brand was the invaluable crown jewel of the company, and "fritos" was challenged as being a generic term. "When a Chicago company came out with 'Jay's fritos,' we spent three years making sure that the Fritos brand did not become a generic term and go the way of formerly famous marks such as aspirin, cellophane, cola, thermos, yo-yo, trampoline, linoleum, or kerosene." In addition, the legality

> In a major case in the early sixties, Mr. Alexander's firm represented Frito-Lay.

of the merger of The Frito Company and H.W. Lay & Co., followed by a merger into PepsiCo in the early sixties, was being challenged by the government based on more than forty prior acquisitions of snack food companies. The Federal Trade Commission alleged monopolization in the corn chip, potato chip, and pretzel product markets. This case presented an opportunity to combine young Miles Alexander's expertise in the trademark and antitrust areas, placing him in a lead role as the young partner coordinating the defense team for the client. Traveling around the country and to

Mexico in PepsiCo and Frito-Lay corporate jets for hearings and depositions, and working with world-renowned senior name partners of firms in Chicago (Hammond Chaffitz), Washington (Jack Howery) and New York (Milton Handler), was a turning point in his career and resulted in these legal areas becoming the primary focus of his future law practice.

He had similar experiences as lead counsel in major cases in the footwear, food, and other industries, and his strong reputation grew.

*Miles Alexander and his wife Elaine with their family in 1968. The children are Paige, 2; David, 8; Michael, 5; and Kent 11.*

He worked with the Blue Cross and Blue Shield Association to create a national uniform license, having been selected in a national search for appropriate counsel. His practice also covered the entertainment arena where a singing telegram business with characters named Super Stud and Wonder Wench were found to infringe the Superman and Wonder Woman trademarks and copyrights. He was similarly contacted by publisher Houghton Mifflin to defend it and an outstanding African-American author, Alice Randall, when the Margaret Mitchell Estate challenged publication of her satirical work *The Wind Done Gone*. Mr. Alexander put together a team of outstanding partners in his firm to successfully resist the challenge.

"Branding has been a big part of my practice. I'm seventy-seven and I'm still asked to stay active because it is such a cutting-edge area of the law. I think if I were doing tax work, I would have retired a long time ago," Mr. Alexander said, adding: "One of the great opportunities in a law firm is working with outstanding younger lawyers. Just as my mentors supported me and would tell clients that I was the right one to use for a case, I can do the same thing for great lawyers who came after me, including Jerre Swann, Virginia Taylor, Joe Beck, Bill Brewster and Ted Davis. This process is all part of the teamwork required to create a continuous flow of talent for great law firms to have one generation succeed another."

Another case meaningful to Mr. Alexander had nothing to do with branding. "A number of years ago, we represented three young women who had been torture victims in Ethiopia. After resettling in the United States, they discovered their torturer working at Colony Square [an office and retail complex in Midtown Atlanta]. We handled that on a *pro bono* basis. We brought him to trial and obtained a judgment that ultimately had him deported to Ethiopia for a trial and conviction there."

Mr. Alexander has also written articles and taught seminars on another topic he is passionate about – "tender loving care of clients." He is an author of an article for the

*New York Law Journal* entitled "Keep Existing Clients Happy" and of a chapter on "Settlement" in a leading legal treatise.

He believes that the most important thing about getting and keeping clients is "caring." "What I mean is that their problems are your problems. You could just be a competent professional and come to work from nine to five, but if you really bleed with the client and understand what they are going through, they know that sense of caring can't be faked and it creates a reciprocal loyalty. It does tear me up if a client is in danger of losing something that is valuable."

One of his first priorities is to try to understand the client's business. "You can't represent someone without understanding what they do. Clients have retained our firm as a result of interviews in which we asked them about their business and their objectives rather than telling them what we could do for them. I had a client who built a very successful communications company called Speakeasy. Its former owner and chief executive was Sandy Linver. As she expanded and her company was becoming an international entity, she was looking for a full-service law firm to represent her. She wrote in one of her books that the reason she chose me and my firm was that other lawyers focused

*Miles Alexander and his wife Elaine with their family at Tybee Island, Georgia.*

on telling her what they could do for her while I was asking questions about her business and what she did. And that was the difference. I didn't do it deliberately to obtain the client, but I was interested in what the business did since I can't tell someone what we can do for them until I understand what they do."

"I am interested in the differences in people and the difference in business, so it is something that comes naturally to me. It is not done in order to obtain clients. I do that at a homeless shelter as readily as with a Fortune 500 executive or opposing counsel. When I meet someone, I ask where they are from and where they went to school and if they have a family. When I am a mediator, I begin the joint session by going around the table and asking clients and lawyers to take a minute or two to give a brief bio of themselves. This often diffuses tensions and identifies common bonds and experiences. It is not inappropriate for a client or even an opponent to become a friend, and to do so one must get to know the individual as a person."

Mr. Alexander also advocates being responsive to clients. "I cannot let a phone call go unreturned. You walk into some lawyers' offices and they have a stack of calls that they are returning at the end of the day. My theory is that if someone is calling, then they need your help now, not at your convenience. If you are in trial, you don't have any choice, but even at breaks in a trial, I'll ask my secretary, Pat Dudek, who has worked with me for thirty years and understands the importance of responsiveness, to refer a client to another lawyer in the firm to make sure their call is returned."

Mr. Alexander believes he stands on the shoulders of great lawyers in his firm who mentored him, including Ernest Rogers and Louis Regenstein, as well as individual younger lawyers he helped recruit to his firm and who now support him. "I think one of the areas that make some people successful and some people not, is a willingness to give credit where credit is due. So many times there are lawyers in my firm who write better than I do, speak better then I do, and can handle many aspects of cases better than I can. If I don't use them rather than doing it myself and if I don't sing their praises, then the clients are going to suffer and my firm will suffer. I think one of the worst things in a profession that anyone can do with respect to their colleagues is take credit for something that someone else has done without acknowledging it. And if you acknowledge the contribution of other lawyers and staff in a law practice, you tend to build confidence in people who work with you and clients know that you will put together the best team to help them in a time of need. By doing so, as you get older, instead of wanting you gone, people want you to stay and help them solve client problems based on your own experience and special strengths."

The talk he gives to new lawyers at his law firm on how to develop clients is called "Tender Loving Care of Clients," which clearly lays out common sense rules for their treatment. One of these is to follow up. After you have advised a client, call and see how it turned out. "How many doctors do you remember because they called you at home after the treatment to find out how you are doing? It's irreplaceable. It's because you care."

Some other points are to: advise clients regularly of changes in the law, recognize your client's idiosyncrasies and review bills as if you were the client reviewing it for reasonableness, keep your client informed of progress or why there is none, provide the client with a realistic analysis of the likelihood of success or failure in litigation or by settlement, and treat everyone with courtesy and respect no matter what their level of responsibility.

## "Lawyers are most effective when they listen. Little is learned while talking."

Mr. Alexander believes that you should make a client part of the team trying to solve the problem. "Recognize that the client often knows more about the problem that you are trying to solve than you do. Don't place yourself above the clients; place yourself with them as part of the team because many times they are most likely to be the source of a solution. They know the intricacies of their business. Lawyers are most effective when they listen. Little is learned while talking. Lawyers are trained to see problems. Someone will give me a set of facts and I will see a whole series of hurdles that may at first blush seem impossible to get over. You have to restrain yourself from focusing only on the hurdles. You also have to focus on how to get over them. Few clients are interested in hearing only why you can't do something; they want to know how to do it legally and ethically."

For example, in a Fotomat Corporation antitrust claim against the Eastman Kodak Company, he defended Fotomat against Kodak's claim to the color yellow as a trademark. Fotomat was buying millions of dollars of film from Kodak but planned to switch to another supplier. "We were twelve million dollars apart in the settlement," he recalled. The solution he came up with called for Kodak to sell its film to Fotomat at cost until the savings equaled the twelve million difference in the settlement proposals.

"This resulted in a win-win solution in which my client, Fotomat, received the full twelve million it sought through pricing discounts, and there was no cost to Kodak."

To obtain new clients, it can be important to get to know other lawyers and people in the legal community. "To know lawyers in other firms and gain their respect will often work to your firm's benefit because when a lawyer has a conflict, he or she may refer the matter to you. Much of what you receive in referrals results from your being on the opposite side and doing outstanding work for your client while conducting yourself in a manner that makes other lawyers understand that you will help their clients, and is evidence to their clients of their own good judgment in choosing you."

He advises young lawyers to become involved in organizations they enjoy – for example, sports, religious affiliated activities, a Boy Scout troop, or activities or organizations dedicated to helping people with medical or financial problems or suffering from discrimination. "If you are active in an organization to meet clients and are not dedicated to that organization's mission, then you are

*Miles Alexander, center, is pictured with four mayors of Atlanta, (l-r) Sam Massell, Andrew Young, Shirley Franklin and Maynard Jackson.*

unlikely to be good at it. People judge you by what you do on a volunteer basis and in your other community activities, and if you don't do what you have undertaken competently, why should they think that you would practice law competently and care about them as a client?"

Mr. Alexander met people in the community in activities ranging from coaching and playing on ball teams to working in a wide range of organizations, including Planned Parenthood, the Anti-Defamation League, American Jewish Committee, area museums, Hands On Atlanta and the American Civil Liberties Union. He also became active in political campaigns and civil rights organizations. In none of these endeavors was meeting clients his motivation.

"I wanted to see good people in government, so I worked on campaigns for various people. I never wanted to run for political office myself, but it was important to me to see people like my best friend, Elliott Levitas, Maynard Jackson (for whom I served as counsel for sixteen years), John Lewis, Andy Young, Sam Massell, and Shirley Franklin, as well as good judges and legislators elected," he said. "I was interested in seeing Atlanta be successful as a biracial city. I felt that Atlanta had more inherent advantages going for it than any city in the United States. Unfortunately, it took a long time for integration to take place in law firms and elsewhere. There was also the gender gap. In the early sixties, The Commerce Club and even the Lawyer's Club were not open to women. I worked hard with others to change those policies. At that time, clubs such as Capital City, Cherokee Town and Country Club, and the Piedmont Driving Club still did not accept women, blacks, or Jews. There have been very positive changes in my lifetime, not only in social integration, but in politics, the professions and education."

Professionally, Mr. Alexander is also heavily involved in Alternative Dispute Resolution. "I would say mediation is one of the most rewarding parts of my practice. Major corporations and individuals prior to or after litigation commences often ask for help to mediate and find a mutually satisfactory solution. It has become a leading area in law practice. It's very satisfying because you may save the parties millions of dollars in litigation costs and/or untold diversion of assets better devoted to the client's mission or bottom line profits. Normally, the mediator is compensated, but I have also served in that role on a pro bono basis when non-profit entities were involved."

## "I have never looked at my watch to see if it is time to go home."

Mr. Alexander has no immediate plans to retire. "My wife would say I was semi-retired because I don't come in every Sunday. I enjoy what I do. I have never looked at my watch to see if it is time to go home. My wife will call after seven o'clock and say, 'Honey, you may not know it, but you are not home.'" When he said that they will be able to take long trips together when he retires, her standard response is, "Wouldn't you rather do it when you're alive?"

Elaine, his wife of more than fifty years, is a leader in the community, but has threatened to bury him with his Blackberry. "She has indicated that she may not wait until I die to do it, because I am always with it. And stopping me from not pulling it out at dinner or a movie is very hard."

But if a young attorney is married and/or has children, he advises him or her to seek some type of balance. "Don't miss the most valuable time of your life because you will never get it back. You can control your hours to some degree, and control your time at work. I remember I came home one night at about seven o'clock and my daughter, Paige, the youngest of our four children, asked what I was doing home so early because I normally didn't make it for supper on school nights. My wife had clipped an article from the *New York Times* that had a study of National Merit Scholars and what they had in common. It wasn't that parents were not divorced, or were wealthy, or where they lived or ethnic or racial background. Far greater than any other common factor, Merit Scholars came from families who ate dinner together. It sort of changed my staying down in the office until nine or ten o'clock. I started coming home for dinner and would go back or just work from home." The practice of doing so, although he refers to it as "far from today's more enlightened joint parenting," has resulted in four outstanding children "who, like me, married above their station," as well as eleven rewarding grandchildren.

Mr. Alexander understands the pressure of billable hours (which did not exist in most Atlanta firms in his formative years of practice) and the challenge it presents for young lawyers to devote the hours to law practice often necessary to achieve partnership. But on the positive side, he points out that law firms make so much money now, they are able to do a good deal of *pro bono* work for myriad worthwhile organizations such as the Atlanta Legal Aid Society and Hands On Atlanta.

# Summary

• Working with a start-up company for little or no compensation can provide a long-term benefit. "Sometimes we were betting that these companies would become successful because they were good business people. Sometimes it was out of friendship because these were people you were close to socially, and they needed assistance and you had the talent or skills to provide it."

• The most important factor in getting and keeping clients is caring. "What I mean is that their problems are your problems. You could just be a competent professional and come to work from 9 to 5, but if you really bleed with the client and understand what they are going through, they know that sense of caring can't be faked and it creates a reciprocal loyalty."

• One of the first steps you should take with a client is try to understand their business. "You can't represent someone without understanding what they do. Clients have retained our firm as a result of interviews in which we asked them about their business and their objectives rather than telling them what we could do for them."

• You have to be responsive to clients. "I cannot let a phone call go unreturned. You walk into some lawyers' offices and they have a stack of calls that they are returning at the end of the day. My theory is that if someone is calling, then they need your help now, not at your convenience."

• Make a client part of the team trying to solve the problem. "Recognize that the client often knows more about the problem that you are trying to solve than you do. Don't place yourself above them; place yourself with them as part of the team because many times they are most likely to be the source of a solution. They know the intricacies of their business. Lawyers are most effective when they listen. Little is learned while talking."

• An important part of being a lawyer is thinking creatively. "Don't get caught up in believing there is only one solution. Look for alternates."

• To obtain new clients, it can be important to get to know other lawyers and people in the legal community. "To know lawyers in other firms and gain their trust will often work to your firm's benefit because when a lawyer has a conflict, he or she may refer the matter to you."

• Lawyers should become involved in organizations that they enjoy. "If you are active in an organization to meet clients and are not dedicated to that organization's mission, then you are unlikely to be good at it. People judge you by what you do on a volunteer basis and in your other community activities, and if you don't do what you have undertaken competently and care, why should they think that you would practice law competently and care about them as a client?"

• Civility to and curiosity about others should be second nature to lawyers. Self-focus and self-indulgence is a dead end, and not an enjoyable way to practice law or live your life.

• Give credit where credit is due. Promoting your colleagues when warranted is not only the right thing to do, but it will gain you their as well as your clients' respect.

# Miles Alexander

Miles Alexander is an internationally known intellectual property lawyer who has served as lead counsel for numerous Fortune 500 companies in major trademark disputes. Mr. Alexander graduated in 1952 from Emory University, where he was a member of Phi Beta Kappa, and from Harvard Law School, cum laude, in 1955. He joined Kilpatrick Stockton after teaching at Harvard Law School and serving two years as a U.S.A.F. Judge Advocate. His commitment to intellectual property practice is demonstrated through the many positions he has held: as a member of the Advisory Council of the J. Thomas McCarthy Center for Intellectual Property and Technology Law at the University of San Francisco, as editor-in-chief of the International Trademark Association's Trademark Reporter, and as a member of the INTA Board of Directors and General Counsel to the International Trademark Association. He was presented with INTA's highest honor, the President's Award; and received Lifetime Achievement Awards from Emory University, Georgia State University, the State Bar of Georgia and its IP Section. He has also been honored by many civil rights organizations and by his partners for many years of service as chair and co-chair of his firm.

Mr. Alexander has written various articles in the trademark and unfair competition fields and has chaired and spoken at seminars and forums sponsored by national and international groups. He is also a member of the American College of Trial Lawyers and authored a chapter on Creative Settlement of Intellectual Property Litigation for a major Clark Boardman treatise. He is a member of the CPR/INTA Panel of "Distinguished Neutrals" and frequently serves as Mediator, Arbitrator and Special Master in major disputes for resolution through ADR procedures. Mr. Alexander is recognized in The Best Lawyers in America® for Corporate, Intellectual Property, Antitrust Law and Alternate Dispute Resolution for 2008 and all prior editions. He also was appointed by the Secretary of Commerce to be the first to Chair the Trademark Public Advisory Committee (2000-2003).

He was also active in two "blue ribbon" bodies of leading intellectual property lawyers: the International Trademark Association's Trademark Review Commission, which drafted the landmark 1989 Lanham Act revisions; and the American Law Institute's committee that drafted the 1995 Restatement of Unfair Competition.

Mr. Alexander was characterized in the 2007 Edition of Chambers as: "incredible – he is an elder statesman of the U.S.I.P. Bar, yet he is always available and is extremely responsive." He is often called upon for his confidential opinions in cutting-edge matters, advising Fortune 500 companies on what to do in trademark-related matters.

Mr. Alexander has been married since 1955 to Elaine Barron Alexander, former executive director of Leadership Atlanta. They have four happily married children, Kent, David, Michael and Paige, who with their spouses, Diane, Deanna, Pamela, and Steve, all accomplished in their own fields, have among them provided eleven grandchildren.

# Griffin Bell

Retired Partner, Senior Counsel
King & Spalding

72nd Attorney General of the United States,
1977-1979

Former United States Circuit Judge
on the Fifth Circuit Court of Appeals

"Everybody is always marketing," said Griffin Bell. "But most lawyers have no idea how to sell anything. They don't teach salesmanship in law school. They don't teach marketing. A lot of people frown on people marketing. When I was a young lawyer we were marketing by doing good work, by going to bar meetings and meeting other lawyers. There has always been some form of marketing in the legal profession."

Judge Bell shares many of the ways he learned about building a law firm during his long and distinguished career, including a few that he learned from Hughes Spalding, son of Jack J. Spalding, who founded King & Spalding in 1885 with Alexander C. King. But one thing he never would do: appear on late-night TV – notwithstanding the impression of a prospective juror in one of his cases.

"We had this case where we represented The Hardaway Company in a suit against the Georgia State Highway Department over a contract to build the Savannah Bridge," he said. "And it was hotly contested and the state wouldn't pay us. It was a lot of money. So we sued the state and were getting ready to try the case in Fulton Superior Court in Atlanta. The state had employed a law firm to represent them and they wanted to qualify the jury by asking them some voir dire questions.

"They asked the judge to ask the prospective jurors – there were about 100 there – if any of them had ever heard of King & Spalding. A lot of them raised their hands. He said, 'Has anyone ever heard of Griffin Bell?' Well, a lot of them raised their hands. Then the lawyer said to the judge, 'I want to ask three or four of these prospective jurors questions about that.' He asked one prospective juror how he had ever heard of me.

"He said, "Do you know him?' The prospective juror said, 'No, I don't know him.' He said, 'How did you ever hear of him?' The prospective juror said, 'I've seen him on late-night television advertising many times.'"

Judge Bell has never appeared on late-night television, but it would be a rare Atlantan who had not heard of this accomplished man. He served as chief of staff to the governor of Georgia, legal advisor to three U.S. presidents, federal appellate judge for fourteen years, attorney general of the United States and managing partner of King & Spalding, just to name a few of his many achievements.

*Being sworn in as the U.S. attorney general*

He joined King & Spalding in 1953 and became managing partner in 1958. He was the tenth lawyer in the firm, which now has more than 800 attorneys in thirteen offices worldwide. Judge Bell said he learned how to sell a law firm from Hughes Spalding, a highly respected attorney who Judge Bell considered a role model, and who knew how to deal with clients.

"The way you sell a law firm is by saying good things about the other lawyers," he said. "Mr. Spalding was a master at that. He employed Furman Smith, who was with a law firm that had broken up. Furman was a genius. So he said to Furman, 'You are now a tax lawyer.' And he told Furman to get the tax code and start studying it because he was going to be a tax lawyer. Then he started telling people that King & Spalding had this brilliant tax lawyer. Well, Furman was a brilliant lawyer, but he didn't know a thing about the tax code when he started. But he became probably the best tax lawyer in this part of the country.

"Mr. Spalding would brag on everybody, saying he had the greatest trial lawyer. That's the way you build up the firm. And he wasn't exaggerating. If you've got a good product, why not tell people about it. That upholds the biblical admonition not to hide your light under the bushel. Mr. Spalding wasn't hiding any lights under the bushel, I can tell you that."

Judge Bell is fond of saying, "It's a sorry dog that won't wag its own tail." He would often brag about the young attorneys at his firm. Then when word got back to them about what Judge Bell was saying, it caused them to want to live up to their press. So his bragging about them became a self-fulfilling prophecy as they tried hard to do what he said they could do.

"My best sales pitch is selling the other lawyers," he said. "We have so many good lawyers at King & Spalding that there is not any problem that we can't handle in some way. If somebody comes to us and says, 'I have a problem, I'm going to turn it over to you, find somebody to get this done,' then we'll get it done. That's my pitch to people.

"If more lawyers thought of selling their partners, more so than themselves, we couldn't handle all the business we would have."

After you get the initial business from the client, you can get more business by handling the matter well, according to Judge Bell. "You get one piece of business from somebody, one matter, and you do a good job, then two things happen. One, they will tell other people about it and second, these same people will bring you more business."

As an example of this, Judge Bell points to Milliken & Company, one of the largest privately held textile and chemical manufacturers in the world. "We got them as a client by handling one case. Judge Robert Bork and I were employed as their special counsel. They had lost a big case and a New York firm had handed it over. As a result of that one case, they moved their legal work from New York to Atlanta."

> "After you get the initial business from the client, you can get more business by handling the matter well."

Another thing he learned from Hughes Spalding is that you have to get out and meet new people. "One time he said, 'I just want to know if anyone ever got any clients by just hanging around the Piedmont Driving Club.' He said that that is not a good way to build up a practice – all those people are already doing business with another firm. And that's true. You've got to get in other circles and meet new people. If all the lawyers did that, you'd be run over with business, probably more than you want."

Fond of hunting and golf, Judge Bell participated in these and several other activities outside the firm. He participated in these because he found them relaxing and he enjoyed getting to know other people. He didn't engage in them to get new clients. But that would often happen.

"It's a marvelous way of getting business. If I'm on a hunting trip, inevitably somebody on the hunting trip has a problem, and they will ask you about it. Most of the time I tell them to go to some other lawyer. A lot of times though, it might be something we can handle so I tell them we can handle that. It's the same way with a lot of business. If they know you, they are more apt to come to you than they are to go to a stranger."

Another way that Judge Bell developed strong relationships with his clients he learned from his father, Adair Cleveland Bell. His law partners would be astounded when Judge Bell would meet somebody, ask them a few questions about their families, and remember the details when he saw them again five years later.

"That's the way of country folk," he said of his childhood growing up on a farm in south Georgia. "They are always asking, 'how's your family?' And usually they give you more information than you really need. In a small town you know who everybody is and who their parents and grandparents were. It's just a way of life.

"I like people and I think people like me. One of my former law partners was a fine person, but he didn't like clients. I had to often remind him that if it wasn't for clients, he wouldn't have anything to do."

Judge Bell served in the military as a company commander in World War II and learned a lot from that experience that he brought to his legal practice. "You are trained to look after your troops – you have to look after your people. And the client is in that category."

*Judge Bell with President John F. Kennedy*

He said that you need to pay a lot of attention to your clients. "The client wants to know that you are thinking about them, you are worried about their business, worried about their problems, and above all, are available for counseling. They also want you to pick out the right lawyers to get their work done. They know law is complex now."

According to Judge Bell, a good law firm can divide lawyers into finders, minders, and grinders, with the most important one being the minder. "Somebody can get a client, or you get them by your own reputation, but you have to spread the work around amongst people who are best at doing their particular thing. That is a minder. The minder is the most important person in the law firm to keep up with the client and make certain they get good service. They will keep using you and recommend you to other people.

"If you think you're just going to do this one job and you're not worried about the whole client and haven't made an effort to learn something about the business, then you're almost like the story of the old man building a cathedral. One man asked one of the workers, 'What are you doing?' and he replied, 'I'm laying brick.' Then he asked another worker the same question, and that man replied, 'I'm building a cathedral.'

From his early days as a lawyer in the firm of Lawton and Cunningham in Savannah, Judge Bell learned about the importance of getting along with your legal community as well. Back in those days, there were about 150 lawyers in the Savannah Bar and many of them would meet at a local saloon at eleven a.m. to drink coffee. They would settle cases there. "That taught me about getting along with other members of the bar," he said. "I know a lot of lawyers and always attended bar association meetings. That way you get to know them and they get to know you."

It was at that firm where Judge Bell first learned that image is important to being a lawyer. "The third day I was in the law firm, I went to the courthouse by myself and tried a case. I don't remember if I won or lost, but one thing I remember about it is the senior partner of the law firm saw me going to the courthouse without a hat on. He told me to get a hat. He said, 'If you're going to be in this law firm you've got to wear a hat.'"

He was also told to wear a jacket, even on the hottest days, after he was caught without one and admonished by an old lawyer, who told him he was a disgrace to the Bar Association.

Years later, during the final days of his service in Washington DC as Attorney General of the United States, Judge Bell ran into a potentially embarrassing situation with a client. King & Spalding had opened a Washington DC office in 1979, and had leased office space near a Subway sandwich shop. Unfortunately, they found out the lease didn't give them permission to go through the front door of the office building; rather they had to enter through the basement, which was leased to Subway.

His client, a four-star general, came to visit and ended up in the sandwich shop. He quickly left because he knew Judge Bell wouldn't have an office in a place like that. King & Spalding has since moved that office to Pennsylvania Avenue.

In his long and distinguished career, Judge Bell worked with several other prominent clients, a list that reads like a personal selection of the finest brand names from a Fortune 100 list. These include E.F. Hutton, Dow Corning and Exxon. But his most important client ever had to wait for a return phone call. Judge Bell was on the golf course when it came.

"I was on the golf course in Sea Island when I got a call from the White House," he said. "They sent a message out on a golf cart to tell me. I said, 'Well we've got three or four holes to play here, so I'll return the call when I get in, unless they left a name.' They didn't leave a name. I'm kind of famous for saying the White House is a building and it can't call anybody. You have to have a name. But the White House operators for years just said the White House is calling. It puts people in fear almost when they get one of these calls. I didn't know who it was, thinking it could have been somebody's secretary.

"When I got in, thirty or forty minutes later, I returned the call. Well, it was the President. I felt very embarrassed, not having taken the call," he laughed. "They didn't say the President is calling. If they had I would have gone in from the golf course."

Judge Bell served as counsel for George H.W. Bush during the Independent Counsel's investigation of the Iran-Contra Affair. Marlin Fitzwater was handling media relations and wanted to issue a long dissertation when President Bush was exonerated.

"We wanted to say nothing even though we won," said Judge Bell, who was in Kennebunkport with the President at the time. "The President never made a statement."

Judge Bell played golf with George H.W. Bush several

*Judge Bell's War Department I.D. (top); with General Colin Powell.*

times, although he said the former president runs around the course. "He wants to make sure he finishes in a very short time. We once played 18 holes in two hours!"

As Attorney General under President Jimmy Carter, a childhood acquaintance from Americus, Georgia, Judge Bell made it a point to say he was the not the president's attorney – he was the people's attorney and never represented Jimmy Carter. In addition to his extensive legal and judicial experience, he also brought something to Washington, D.C. that was desperately needed: a sense of humor.

*Judge Bell with President George H.W. Bush (top); a photo of him in the oval office, signed by President Bush.*

To Griffin Bell – with Respect always and high personal regard. Geo Bush

"No one had laughed in Washington for years when I got there," he said. "I've always said that to be a good lawyer, you've got to have a good sense of humor, to break the tension if for nothing else." Judge Bell is known for his wit and has been called a cross between Mark Twain and John Marshall.

However, in the spirit of marketing a good product, he nearly got himself and a *Newsweek* reporter in a lot of trouble. It all started with a hunting trip with his friend and law partner, Charles Kirbo, who was serving as Jimmy Carter's closest advisor.

"Charlie Kirbo and I were quail hunting in south Georgia one day, on his land near Bainbridge, Georgia. This farmer came to where we were hunting and said that he had some fresh sausage and that he was able to find some rooster pepper and it really made it taste better. Charlie didn't know what rooster pepper was, nor did I. It's a hot pepper about the size of your little finger.

"So Charlie and I started telling people about this rooster pepper sausage. We acted as if it were an aphrodisiac. It created great curiosity. People wanted to know where to get it. I kept telling this story in Washington. Finally this reporter for *Newsweek*, Elaine Shannon, who is from Gainesville, Georgia, wrote a story in the magazine about rooster pepper sausage. Her bosses inquired about it and they finally decided it was a hoax. So they were thinking about firing her.

"She called me up crying and said she was about to lose her job. Well I thought it was terrible they thought it's a hoax so I called Justice Bob Jordon of the Georgia Supreme Court. I knew he commuted from Talbotton, Georgia, near Columbus, to Atlanta every day. There's a place that sells sausage in Harrelson, Georgia on the way. So I asked him to get some rooster pepper, take it down there, get them to grind it up and put it in some sausage. Then I asked him to ship some up to me by Delta Dash, as I needed it the next day.

"He knew about the joke. So he shipped it up there and I had a wine and hors d'oeuvres party at the press office at the Justice Department the next day. We had the rooster pepper sausage cut up and cooked at the dining room and served on toothpicks.

All these press people, there were about fifty, were saying how good it was, and we also leaked it out that it was an aphrodisiac. Some of the women jokingly wanted to go home and find their husbands."

But the story doesn't end there. President Carter heard about it and wanted to taste it himself. "He called me and said he wanted to have some at the White House. 'But you can't send it through Secret Service because they will eat it,' the president said. 'They eat everything people send me.' Meanwhile, one of the people at the

> "I long ago decided I wasn't going to write the Declaration of Independence. So I am fulfilled by my legal career."

tasting was the food editor at the *Washington Post*. So that night they had us on *NBC Evening News* talking about this fine sausage. I had people calling me wanting to get the recipe, offering me a royalty. I told Kirbo that we're going to be put in prison before it's over with, about this hoax we made up.

"I got the sausage in for the president and I called and told him. He said, 'How are you going to get it over here? Are you going to bring it?' I said, 'No, I'm going to send my car over there to Pennsylvania Avenue. Send Kirbo down to the fence. He may need to put on a trench coat or something. And my driver is going to hand the sausage to him through the fence.' So that all worked out and the president called me and said it was the best sausage he ever tasted."

That is just another example of how Judge Bell was able to solve problems, a skill highly valued by his clients. "What being a lawyer really amounts to is being a problem solver. Most everybody that comes to you has a problem. And they really wouldn't need you if they could solve the problem themselves. We have to be problem solvers."

In the end, Judge Bell said being a lawyer is about being fulfilled in this multifaceted profession. "Thomas Jefferson was quite a great lawyer until he was about 30 years old. Then he sold his practice. He said he wasn't being fulfilled. So he got in to the Continental Congress and wrote the Declaration of Independence. He was fulfilled by writing the Declaration of Independence.

"I long ago decided I wasn't going to write the Declaration of Independence. So I am fulfilled by my legal career."

# Summary

• The best way to sell a law firm is to sell the attorneys you work with. "If more lawyers thought of selling their partners, more so than themselves, they couldn't handle all the business they would have."

• After you get the initial business from a client, you can get more business by handling the matter well. "You get one piece of business from somebody, one matter, and you do a good job, then two things happen. One, they will tell other people about it and second, these same people will bring you more business."

• You have to get out and meet new people. "One time Hughes Spalding said, 'I just want to know if anyone ever got any clients by just hanging around the Piedmont Driving Club.' He said that that is not a good way to build up a practice – all those people are already doing business with another firm."

• Engage in activities you enjoy outside the law firm. "It's a marvelous way of getting business. If I'm on a hunting trip, inevitably somebody on the hunting trip has a problem, and they will ask me about it. I tell them we can handle that. It's the same way with a lot of business. If they know you, they are more apt to come to you than they are to go to a stranger."

• Pay a lot of attention to your clients. "The client wants to know that you are thinking about them, you are worried about their business, worried about their problems and above all, the client wants you to be available for counseling."

• A good law firm can divide lawyers into finders, minders, and grinders, with the most important one being the minder. "The minder is the most important person in the law firm to keep up with the client and make certain they get good service."

# Griffin Bell

*Griffin B. Bell is a senior counsel in the law firm of King & Spalding LLP in Atlanta.*

*Judge Bell was born in Americus, Georgia, on October 31, 1918, and attended public schools and Georgia Southwestern College. From 1941 to 1946, he served in the U.S. Army, attaining the rank of major. In 1948, he graduated cum laude from Mercer University Law School in Macon with an LL.B. degree. He has received the Order of the Coif from Vanderbilt Law School and honorary degrees from Mercer University and several other colleges and universities.*

*From 1948 to 1961, he practiced law in Georgia, joining King & Spalding in 1953 and becoming its managing partner in 1958. He served as senior partner until January 1, 2004, at which time he became senior counsel for the firm.*

*Judge Bell was appointed by President John F. Kennedy to the U.S. Court of Appeals for the Fifth Circuit in 1961. Judge Bell served on the Fifth Circuit for 15 years until 1976, and during that time was a director of the Federal Judicial Center. In December 1976, President Jimmy Carter nominated him to become the seventy-second Attorney General of the United States. Judge Bell received the oath of office from Chief Justice Warren E. Burger in January 1977 and served as Attorney General until August 1979.*

*During 1980, Judge Bell led the American delegation to the Conference on Security and Cooperation in Europe, held in Madrid. In 1981, he served as co-chairman of the Attorney General's National Task Force on Violent Crime. He received the Thomas Jefferson Memorial Foundation Award in 1984 for excellence in law.*

*From 1985 to 1986, Judge Bell served as president of the American College of Trial Lawyers. From 1985 to 1987, he served on the Secretary of State's Advisory Committee on South Africa. He also was a director of the Ethics Resource Center for several years and in 1986 served as its chairman of the board. From 1986 to 1989, Judge Bell served as a member of the Board of Trustees of the Foundation for the Commemoration of the United States Constitution. In 1989, he accepted an appointment as vice chairman of President George H.W. Bush's Commission on Federal Ethics Law Reform. During the Independent Counsel's investigation of the Iran-Contra Affair, Judge Bell represented President Bush.*

*In his private practice, Judge Bell has represented clients in all phases of trial and appellate litigation. He has conducted numerous investigations, including internal reviews for E.F. Hutton's board of directors concerning fraud charges, and an independent review of the Exxon Valdez oil spill in Alaska commissioned by Exxon Corporation's board of directors.*

*Judge Bell continues to practice law and is active in issues involving the U.S. Constitution and the nation's judicial system. In 2002, Judge Bell served on Secretary Donald Rumsfeld's ad hoc Advisory Committee on new rules governing military tribunals. He also served on the Webster Commission, which in March 2002 issued its report on FBI security programs and Russian spy Robert Hanssen. In 2003, he served on the Technology and Privacy Advisory Committee for the Department of Defense and chaired a Study Group regarding the FBI's Office of Professional Responsibility. He was also selected by the Defense Department to be a member of the Review Panel for Military Commissions and served as chief judge until resigning in November 2007.*

# Emmet Bondurant

Partner
Bondurant Mixson & Elmore

Emmet Bondurant believes in building a legal practice through hard work and performance. "The way we built our firm was by doing first-class legal work. We work hard and do well and other people notice," he said. "A vast percentage of my own work comes from referral by other lawyers. We've never done any advertising."

Bondurant Mixson & Elmore's client strategy is straightforward. "The principle thing we do with all of our client relationships is to do the best possible job that we can in the litigation. If the clients feel they are getting first-class service at a reasonable price, we hope they will come back."

He acknowledges that building a practice this way is a slow process. "It takes a lot of time and effort so that people in the community and other lawyers in particular who are put in a position to be decision makers acquire enough confidence in you to recommend you to someone else or to hire you themselves when they have a problem. And that's the way we prefer to do it."

Mr. Bondurant's firm handles only litigation, particularly complex commercial matters. "We do both plaintiffs' work and defendants' work. Unlike many firms that feel that they have to be either a plaintiffs' or defendants' firm, we never felt that was the case. We are perfectly comfortable being either, depending on the case." Mr. Bondurant added, "We are the closest thing you can come to being English barristers in the sense that most of our clients are people who come to us as either defendants or plaintiffs when they have a particular crisis. And when they're through they'll go back to wherever they're generally represented. We do not compete with the large firms that represent them regularly for other kinds of business."

This boutique law firm of just seventeen partners often receives referrals from other lawyers, including those who were on the other side in cases and who have a conflict in representing a client. "They feel comfortable in referring a client to us because they know we're not going to try to steal the client and that we will do an excellent job," Mr. Bondurant said.

Bondurant, Mixson, & Elmore values its professional independence and isn't afraid to litigate against large corporations. The firm won a $454 million verdict against a Fortune 100 company, the largest verdict in Georgia history, and achieved a settlement valued at over $192 million for a class of plaintiffs in a race discrimination lawsuit against The Coca-Cola Company, which was the largest settlement of a private discrimination suit. Mr. Bondurant was once quoted as saying, "If you are afraid to represent underdogs in litigation, you do not belong in the legal profession." Mr. Bondurant has also prevailed on the defense side of cases, successfully representing Weyerhaeuser Co. in overturning a $458 million judgment on appeal, and obtaining a complete defense verdict for a client that was named among the *National Law Journal's* top ten defense verdicts.

Mr. Bondurant, who was recognized as one of the top ten trial lawyers in the country by the *National Law Journal* in 2001, and received the highest number of votes in the Super Lawyers poll for the past five years, showed his brilliance in the legal profession at a young age. He argued his first case in the United States Supreme Court in 1962, when he was just twenty-six years old.

After graduating from law school at the University of Georgia in 1960, Mr. Bondurant served as a law clerk for the Honorable Clement F. Haynsworth Jr., who was then relatively new to the United States Court of Appeals for the Fourth Circuit, and later became

*Emmet Bondurant argued his first case in the United States Supreme Court in 1962, when he was just twenty-six years old.*

Chief Judge. "Because I had an interest in constitutional law I applied to Harvard for a fellowship and frankly, with his recommendation, got one. It paid all of $2,200 a year but covered the tuition, which tells you how long ago that was. I spent a year there taking a wide variety of courses including a constitutional litigation seminar under Paul Freund, who was one of the brightest minds in legal circles."

Mr. Bondurant spent his fellowship year devoted almost exclusively to reapportionment issues. Later that year, Mr. Bondurant moved to Atlanta where he worked for Kilpatrick, Cody, Rogers, McClatchey and Regenstein, the predecessor firm to Kilpatrick Stockton. Because of Mr. Bondurant's previous work on reapportionment issues he was asked to work on several pending cases that ultimately went to the United States Supreme Court, including the challenge to congressional districts in the case of

*Wesberry v. Sanders* (376 U.S. 1 (1964)), and the challenge to reapportionment of the Georgia General Assembly in *Fortson v. Toombs* (379 U.S. 621 (1965)). "I had spent a vast portion of the previous year on those issues," he said. "I had read every case in the Western Hemisphere – and maybe beyond – that dealt with the subject, so I had a head start on most people in working on those cases."

While at Kilpatrick, Mr. Bondurant had a full workload but spent a lot of time doing pro bono work. "Those were the days in which there were no pro bono departments and you were not given time off for non-paying litigation, no matter how useful and no matter how much public interest there may have been, so I handled those during my free time." A pro bono department in a law firm is a relatively recent innovation, particularly in Atlanta. "I give the Kilpatrick firm a great deal of credit for allowing me to take on controversial litigation. Had I been at any other major law firm in Atlanta, I probably would not have been allowed to take these cases. I took on a lot of controversial cases pro bono because I was interested in the issues and felt it was important and a good use of my time."

> A pro bono department in a law firm is a relatively recent innovation, particularly in Atlanta.

For example, while at Kilpatrick, Mr. Bondurant also worked on court appointed criminal cases, which he got to argue before the United States Court of Appeals for the Fourth Circuit. "In the ordinary course of a business firm's practice, it would not be uncommon that people would be there for ten to fifteen years before they would ever have the responsibility of a paying case in the Court of Appeals," he said. "I had acquired experience that many people senior to me had not had because of my pro bono work." These cases also allowed him to be in charge of a case from start to finish.

"I knew at the time that I was doing things that contemporaries at other firms would not have been allowed or dared to do. And nobody ever said a cross word to me about having done them." Mr. Bondurant still had to do his share of billable work in addition to his pro bono work. "I arrived around eight o'clock in the morning and I worked until about nine-thirty or ten o'clock at night."

Mr. Bondurant was always attracted to litigation because, "It's more fun than any other practice of law," he said. "Litigation is where all the disputes get resolved. Obviously I've done a lot of public policy litigation and litigation is frequently the only mechanism for getting those disputes resolved in a way that makes any sense or allows for a constructive result."

Many of Mr. Bondurant's cases have been considered controversial, including the reapportionment cases. He also worked on a case in which he challenged the oath that the State required everyone in the university system to take (*Georgia Conf. of American Ass'n of Univ. Professors v. Bd. of Regents, 246 F. Supp. 553 (1965)*). "These were plainly unconstitutional," he said. "I got zero criticism within the firm, although the then-chief justice of the Georgia Supreme Court went on television and said that he had fought in World War I and he had signed the oath, and he thought that all the university professors who wouldn't sign it should be deported. Ordinarily in a business firm you don't go out of your way to alienate the chief justice of the Georgia Supreme Court."

Another important case Mr. Bondurant worked on was a gender discrimination case that went to the U.S. Supreme Court (*Hishon v. King & Spalding*, 467 U.S. 69 (1984)). Elizabeth Hishon was an associate at the prestigious Atlanta law firm of King & Spalding, who was twice considered and rejected for partnership, then fired in 1979. The court ruled unanimously that Title VII was applicable to partnerships and therefore Hishon had a right to sue for alleged discrimination. After that decision the parties settled the suit out of court. "It was clearly a controversial thing at the time, but it was clearly the right thing to do," said Mr. Bondurant.

Mr. Bondurant also successfully handled the death penalty appeal of Gary Nelson after he was convicted, based on circumstantial evidence, of the murder of a young girl in Savannah in 1978. Ultimately, the Georgia Supreme Court held that prosecutors in the case suppressed evidence that would have cleared Mr. Nelson of the charges (*Nelson v. Zant*, 261 Ga. 358 (1991)).

Although Mr. Bondurant was involved in controversial cases during his entire career, it has not deterred clients from hiring him. "We take the view that we do not let clients tell us who we can represent," he said. "And the fact that a client may be offended by the fact that I represented Gary Nelson or Betsy Hishon or any number of other people is not something that factors into whether we take those cases. If they're important, particularly pro bono cases, the rule is if there's no conflict of interest with a client and we're willing to commit the time, then we take the case. And once we take the case, it becomes as important as any other firm case." He added, "You simply can't let public perception dictate what you choose to do professionally or how you choose to do it, assuming you're doing it the right way and happen to believe in it." Mr. Bondurant is also currently representing the Democratic Party of Georgia in its state court challenge to the constitutionality of the state's voter identification law.

Another example of Mr. Bondurant's commitment to pro bono work is his firm's representation of Ahmad Errachidi, a Moroccan citizen who was in an automobile accident in Pakistan and wound up being incarcerated at Guantánamo Bay. "We believe he was sold by the Pakistan security forces to the CIA for a bounty and was then taken to Afghanistan and held at one of the many secret bases there where he was tortured, then taken to Guantanamo Bay and held for five years. He never had a trial or went before a judge and there was no evidence against him," Mr. Bondurant said. "We became involved with the case because the American College of Trial Lawyers sent out a notice saying that the Center for Constitutional Rights in New York was looking for representation for people like Mr. Errachidi. I would have volunteered for those cases years earlier had I been aware of an avenue to do it."

> ## Although Mr. Bondurant was involved in controversial cases his entire career, it has not deterred clients from hiring him.

Unfortunately Mr. Bondurant did not get to try the Errachidi case. "The courts in Washington abdicated their judicial responsibility and essentially did nothing in the cases while the government stalled, appealing one case after another. They did it to hundreds of detainees and our client was one of them. We spent a lot of time on the legal theories and everything else, and would have liked very much to have tried it, but we could never get a hearing. We were basically relegated to the sidelines. It was frustrating to me then and it is still frustrating to me now. I would very much have liked to litigate the case."

Mr. Bondurant and his partner, Ronan Doherty, filed a *habeas corpus* petition in the District of Columbia in the Errachidi matter. They also worked with Clive Stafford Smith, a noted British death penalty lawyer who has represented several Guantanamo detainees. "The government's position with reference to all of the Guantánamo Bay inmates is the most serious threat to fundamental constitutional rights in this country at least since the Civil War. But at least in the case of the Civil War, Congress suspended the writ of *habeas corpus*. Here President Bush is acting on his own." Eventually, even the government admitted that there was no reason to continue holding Mr. Errachidi. Many months later, with the help of the Carter Center in Atlanta, Mr. Errachidi was released to Morocco, where he was freed by the Moroccan government and has been reunited with his wife, two young sons, and the rest of his family.

With his reputation, Mr. Bondurant can choose which clients he wishes to represent. "Sometimes I conclude that I simply don't want to represent them," he said. "You try to get a sense of what the client is like. It doesn't have as much to do with the merits as it does with the character of the client. I met with one man and whenever he came to a fork in the road and he had the chance to do something honest or dishonest, he unerringly chose the dishonest route. At the interview, I declined to represent him. He insisted on knowing why, so I told him."

Mr. Bondurant's advice is this, "If you interview a client, no matter how big the client may be, or how big the fees are that might be involved, if you get that sense of them that they have the unerring sense to do the dishonest thing or that they are of a personality that no matter what you do for them they will be dissatisfied, my advice is to decline the representation."

He also refers cases to other lawyers outside the firm where he feels there are people better qualified than he is to represent them, such as in domestic matters. "In those instances I try to refer them to someone who is more expert in a particular field than we are and who I feel can do a better job for them."

As far as advice for young attorneys looking to build a career, Mr. Bondurant suggests that they become active in the community in an area in which they believe. "I've chaired Common Cause, an organization that will alienate some people and attract others. It's worth doing in and of itself because of its intrinsic value."

With his passionate beliefs, it is no surprise that he has also been involved with the

*Mr. Bondurant's client Gary Nelson crocheted this sweater for Mr. Bondurant while on death row.*

Atlanta Legal Aid Society. Mr. Bondurant served as president in 1970 and is still involved in fundraising.

"Atlanta Legal Aid is clearly one of the leading legal aid societies in the country and has been for the last thirty years," he said.

Mr. Bondurant also advises young attorneys to choose a law firm very carefully and once they have done so to take responsibility for themselves. He acknowledges that the practice of law has changed and believes that it is cyclical. "The lawyers who you recruited in the late sixties and the early seventies were very idealistic, and in the eighties they were dreadfully materialistic. It was the era of greed is good, how much are you going to pay me, how big a house can I get, how soon can I join a country club kind of thing. There was very little interest in pro bono work or something that wasn't going to pay them directly. In the nineties that started to shift back in the other direction as firms have gotten much larger."

*A favorite vacation spot is Alaska, where Emmet Bondurant poses with a fish he caught there.*

"On the positive side, the large firms have established pro bono departments and have devoted very significant resources to doing things that twenty years ago many large firms in Atlanta would never have allowed lawyers to do. On the other hand, they are putting tremendous pressure on young lawyers for billable hours, which essentially precludes people who are not assigned to the pro bono departments from going out and taking on a cause of their own, so I'm glad I'm on this side of the legal profession in my career and not at the other end. I really was fortunate with Kilpatrick."

At an age when many of his contemporaries are lounging on their fishing boats or lining up their next tee time, Mr. Bondurant keeps a full schedule, with no desire to retire any time soon. The former marathoner and lifelong swimmer exercises daily, hitting the pool to swim laps at five-thirty before putting in a full day at the office.

"I enjoy fishing, but I hate golf," he said. "If you played as badly as I did you would understand why. I play once a year at the firm outing, and that holds me for the next year. Other people play golf. I litigate cases."

# Summary

- Do first-class legal work. "We work hard and do well and other people notice," he said. "A vast percentage of my own work comes from referrals by other lawyers."

- Do pro bono work to get more experience. "In the ordinary course of events at the firm, even if you were writing a brief, you were working for a more senior person. You were not in charge of the case. Big people make decisions that overrule little people. In pro bono cases I was in charge from start to finish. It was my case and my responsibility."

- Do not take on a client if it is not a good fit for you or the firm. "If you interview a client, no matter how big the client may be, or how big the fees are that might be involved, if you get that sense of them that they have the unerring sense to do the dishonest thing or that they are of a personality that no matter what you do for them they will be dissatisfied, my advice is to decline the representation."

- Become active in your community in an area that you are interested in, which will help you meet people in the community.

- Find the right firm for you. "I was extraordinarily fortunate to find the right firm. It is critical to find a good match when you are looking for a firm."

# Emmet Bondurant

*Emmet Bondurant has been a trial lawyer for more than forty-five years. Although he has specialized in antitrust law, he has also represented both plaintiffs and defendants in a wide variety of other areas including patent, securities, trade secret, professional malpractice and complex corporate disputes in federal and state trial and appellate courts.*

*He argued his first case in the U.S. Supreme Court in 1962, when he was twenty-six. He received a Trial Lawyer of the Year Award from the Georgia Chapter of the American Board of Trial Advocacy in 1992, and in 2001, he was recognized by the* National Law Journal *as one of the top ten trial lawyers in the United States.*

*He is a member of both the American College of Trial Lawyers and the American Academy of Appellate Lawyers and currently serves as a member of the National Governing Board of Common Cause, the Anti-Defamation League, Southeastern Regional Board, and the Board of Counselors of The Carter Center. He was one of four editors of the 1975 edition of Antitrust Law Development published by the Antitrust Section of the ABA.*

*Mr. Bondurant's career has included a strong commitment to community service and pro bono litigation, including death penalty, habeas corpus, reapportionment, and other civil rights and constitutional cases. He has served as chairman of the Atlanta Charter Commission (1972-74); president and a director of the Atlanta Legal Aid Society; a member of the Executive Committee of the Joseph Henry Lumpkin and Logan E. Bleckley American Inns of Court, a trustee of the American Inns of Court Foundation; as chairman and a member of the Board of Common Cause Georgia; chairman of the Georgia Public Defender Standards Council (2003-2007); and as a director and chairman of the Georgia Appellate Practice Education & Resource Center.*

# Bobby Lee Cook

Partner
Cook & Connelly

**K**nown as one of the best trial lawyers in the South and widely believed to be the inspiration for the television character Matlock, Bobby Lee Cook has been described as a wizard in the courtroom, and a mixture of Patrick Henry, Thomas Jefferson, Abraham Lincoln, and Shakespeare. He is in a word, legendary.

Working out of his small office in Summerville, Georgia, Mr. Cook has defended those accused of such crimes as arson, murder, moon shining and even a banker who was accused of making four billion dollars in loans to Saddam Hussein's regime. He maintains a large civil practice as well, with his firm, Cook & Connelly, and enjoys the mix.

"I don't consider myself to be a specialist," he said. "I'm somewhat of a generalist. I've always labored under the impression that a good lawyer, that a highly skilled and competent lawyer, can learn to try any type of case, and I don't think that's bragging. That's not done much anymore. There are some types of cases that we don't do, like highly sophisticated security cases or tax cases. But we do a little bit of everything." There are just three lawyers in his firm, which he said is just enough. "Sometimes I think it might be too many," he said laughing.

"The media pays the most attention to criminal cases. They have a sensational edge to them, much more than the civil cases, but our civil practice has been just as extensive as our criminal practice. We have had a very large civil practice over a long period of time – fifty-nine years."

But whether he is involved in a civil or criminal case, Mr. Cook's principles for treating all clients – rich, poor, unknown, famous, or infamous – remain the same: be civil with your clients, be truthful to your clients, stay in the driver's seat, return phone calls, have a dedicated work ethic and keep to your timetables.

"You've got to be civil with people," he said. "You've got to be understanding of their problems. You deal with people who are sophisticated, you deal with uneducated people, you deal with people who are less understanding than others. But you've got to listen. And if you learn to listen, you'll learn a lot. I tried to be understanding of their problems and to be helpful with their problems."

> Be civil with your clients, be truthful to your clients, stay in the driver's seat, return phone calls, have a dedicated work ethic and keep to your timetables.

Mr. Cook believes being honest with a client is of utmost importance. "It's essential, overwhelmingly essential, for lawyers to be absolutely, totally, critically honest with their clients. Everybody wants to hear good news. You cannot just tell your client what he or she wants to hear. We want to be optimistic but you can't give good news all the time. On the civil side, people come in and they've lost a son in an airplane crash or an automobile accident. But you can't tell them that a jury is going to give them five million dollars. You can't tell them that because that's not the truth and we don't have that much foresight. About all you can do is if you see that it's a good case, you can tell them that you believe that it's a good case and that you'll do the best that you can, but there are so many factors involved that you can't give the good news that everybody wants to hear."

A lawyer has to control the situation. "You've got to have absolute loyalty to your client and also have to take control of the situation, not in an arrogant or overreaching way, but you've got to be in the driver's seat. If you aren't, it can get away from you in a hurry."

As a nationally famous attorney, Mr. Cook receives phone calls from all types of people, and he returns them all. "I always return all of my calls. I get calls from people I don't know, and for half of them there's nothing I can do. I get a call from somebody from south Georgia or south Alabama about some matter. But I'm eighty-one years old and I'm not going to south Alabama to try a case. But I talk to them. I'm civil with them. Returning calls is a very important thing in the law practice. You never can get too big for your britches. You certainly can be self-assured but there's a difference between being self-assured or confident and being arrogant."

After nearly six decades of practicing law, Mr. Cook has observed a thing or two. One of those is that to be a good lawyer you have to work hard. "Some of us tend to be a little lazy. Good lawyers, successful lawyers, have a dedicated work ethic and have a timetable for everything. And you've got to keep your eye on what you're doing and look after your business in a timely fashion. And you've got to really believe in what you're doing. You've got to have a well-settled belief that what you're doing is a little more than just making a living. You've got to feel like you're making some contribution – for institutional change."

A good trial lawyer also has to know how to speak in front of people. "If you're trying cases to the jury or to the court, you've got to know how to talk. We all find our way of saying things. No one can be an Emmet Bondurant. I can't copy Emmet or Frank

Love. We all eventually find our style, and if you do try to copy somebody, usually it's a mistake. But of course we all learn from each other."

Mr. Cook's legal practice had rather humble beginnings. Born in the nearby town of Lyerly, Georgia, Mr. Cook started practice in Summerville after attending law school at Vanderbilt University. He took the bar exam prior to graduating, passed it and started his practice. He rented two small rooms above the drugstore and began his career with appointed cases in the circuit and state courts. It was a great way to get a practice started – except that these cases didn't pay anything.

"At that time, lawyers who were appointed to defend criminal cases did not receive any fees or expense whatsoever and it was that way for many years. It was also like that in the federal system. So most of the cases that I had to begin with were appointed cases with no remuneration. And then very quickly I started picking up some business from the local bootleggers and the local moonshiners. In fact, back during the fifties and the sixties, the largest industry in northwest Georgia, northeast Georgia, east Tennessee, and east Alabama was the illegal liquor industry. And many of those cases paid pretty well. It's hard to believe, looking back, but I even made a living the first year of the practice. It wasn't a hell of a lot compared to what lawyers consider money today. As time progressed, I tried lots of cases, one after another. I started winning a lot of cases. And the business started coming."

Mr. Cook was attracted to criminal law because of the importance of the constitutional rights of individuals that are involved. "You deal with the freedoms of individuals, and that has a very attractive quality to me. To have a human life in your hands, professionally, is a very heavy-weighted situation. Or to have someone's liberty in your hands, so to speak, is equally about as serious as you can get. To me, it is a lot easier dealing with someone's money or property than it is dealing with someone's liberty or life."

Although he handled dozens of murder cases, he still remembers his first. A local man had killed his brother in an argument over a turnip patch. "It was sort of a Cain and Abel situation. I won that case, and then I started getting hired for murder cases and bootleg cases and all types of criminal cases and then started getting civil business."

Summerville isn't too large – the current population is 5,000 – and word soon spread that Mr. Cook was winning

*Bobby Lee Cook in the early years of his legal career, surrounded by books. "I'm the only damn fool who buys law books anymore," he said.*

cases. "I won some cases in the beginning of my career, a lot of cases that would be considered insignificant now, but word gets out, and I started trying cases one after another. And you know, people like a winner."

In the days before TV was widespread, his reputation grew by word of mouth. "It's a slow, gradual process. I don't think there's any magic wand that you can wave, but you build up a reputation for being competent and good and sometimes winning."

Word has indeed gotten out about several of Mr. Cook's more infamous clients, many of whom were involved in trials covered extensively in the press, sometimes internationally. He defended Fred Tokars, who was charged with ordering the shotgun slaying of his wife in front of their two children in 1992. He argued for a new trial for Wayne Williams, convicted in the missing and murdered children cases that took place in Atlanta between 1979 and 1981. He defended porn king Michael Thevis in a RICO case and former Congressman Pat Swindall in a perjury case. He defended Savannah businessman Jim Williams, who was accused of killing Danny Hansford, a trial that was made famous by the book and movie *Midnight in the Garden of Good and Evil*.

Mr. Cook is often found on the plaintiff's side as well. He filed a fifteen million dollar libel suit on behalf of the widow and family of soul singer Otis Redding against author Scott Freeman for alleged rumors in his book *Otis! The Otis Redding Story*. Asked what his clients were seeking with the lawsuit, Mr. Cook responded, "a hell of a lot of money."

Mr. Cook waves enthusiastically during a meeting of the National Association of Claimants' Compensation Attorneys, (which later merged and is now the American Association for Justice), held in Havana a few months after the Cuban Revolution of 1959.

But it isn't always about money for Mr. Cook, although his services generally require a hefty fee. "Particularly in the criminal field, I have accepted some cases pro bono where I had a great feeling that a tremendous principle – constitutional or otherwise – was involved, and that it needed me or someone like me in the profession to do something about it. So you do that without regard to money. Then there are those cases that do not involve a great principle or a great right and wrong that you have to judge on the economic scale. You have to ask yourself, if I get into this case, how much of my time is it going to take? Is it worthwhile for the client for me to charge a fee of X dollars? So you have to make an economic judgment. After all, as great as we think we are in terms of taking care of the world, there is a basic economic principle in the law practice."

Mr. Cook, who declares himself a book person, said that keeping up his law library alone costs him one hundred thousand dollars a year. "Though, of course, lawyers don't buy books anymore. I'm the only damn fool that buys them. As long as I'm here I'm going to keep up the library. If I can't keep it up, I'll quit. But there are different ways of judging whether or not to take a case."

One case he took for no fee was that of bank manager Christopher M. Drogoul. Mr. Drogoul was accused of making four billion dollars in unsecured loans to Saddam Hussein's regime before the invasion of Kuwait, a scandal that came to be known as Iraqgate.

"During the years of Saddam Hussein, when Iraq was fighting Iran, the bank had loaned Iraq several billions of dollars in violation of American banking laws. Two days after the first Iraq war ended, the Bush administration sent the Justice Department in and they made a raid on the bank and arrested Drogoul and other officers. The thrust of the case that we were ultimately able to show was that Drogoul was doing exactly what the CIA and the American government had covertly approved. And it was all just a hell of a mess. We finally prevailed after about six weeks in front of Judge Marvin Shoob. The case received worldwide publicity, and I didn't get a nickel out of it.

## Through the years Mr. Cook has kept people out of prison, saved them money, and made them millions of dollars.

"Some things you do because you feel that there is a high principle involved, that somebody – pardon the expression – that somebody needs to be kicked in the butt occasionally, when they are doing things they have no right to do."

Through the years Mr. Cook has kept people out of prison, saved them money and made them millions of dollars. But the case he is most proud of is a murder case. In 1972, Drs. Rozina and Warren Matthews were murdered in their home in Marietta, Georgia. Seven people were arrested, tried, and convicted on the basis of the testimony of a drug abuser and prostitute, with one receiving the death penalty. "All of the cases went to the Georgia Supreme Court. All of them were affirmed. I ultimately went into the Federal Court under a federal *habeas corpus*. We were able to establish, beyond any doubt, that these people were totally innocent and that the district attorney and the law enforcement officers had set them up. It was the most important *habeas corpus* decision in this part of the country for a long time, so I'm real proud of that. That was a case that I spent over one hundred thousand dollars of my own money doing what I thought needed to be done."

Mr. Cook believes that to be a successful trial lawyer, you have to be able to read people. "That doesn't mean you don't make mistakes," he said. "We're not talking about an absolute science, but you need to be a good reader of people in the selection of a jury. You're addressing the jury and you've got to have a feel for the people that you're talking to, whether they are receptive to what you're about to say."

An example of his ability to read people is the jury selection for the trial of C. H. Butcher, a prominent banker in Tennessee who was indicted for bank fraud. No one thought Mr. Cook could win, but after a six-week trial, the jury found Mr. Butcher not guilty on all counts.

"I had my partner, my son-in-law who died in 2007, and my associate with me in Chattanooga. We had this little lady as a prospective juror, who was about eighty-two, and they said, 'You don't want to take her, do you?' And I said, 'Yeah, I'm going to take her. I like her. She's got a little twinkle in her eye, and I think she would be ideal for this case. I think she'd like C.H.' They were both opposed to it.

"When the case was over, the television cameras were set up outside the court-room. It was Saturday night, about ten o'clock outside the federal building in Chattanooga, and the U.S. attorney thought he had the case won. He was all dressed up – got him a new suit on and he was ready to go out in front of the cameras. When the jury came back, he was crestfallen and went out the back of the courthouse. I went out the front. And this little lady, who was the spokesperson for the jury, was standing out there in front of the cameras. I went out, and they wanted me to say a few words. I went up the camera, and this little eighty-two-year-old lady came up and hugged my neck and said,

*Bobby Lee Cook in his office in Summerville, Georgia.*

'Mr. Bobby Lee, I was with you from the first day.'"

Mr. Cook said that one of the biggest mistakes a lawyer can make is to misjudge the intelligence of a jury. "You can have a jury with someone who's a cotton picker, you've got somebody who works up at the mill at Mount Vernon, you've got a lady who works as a teller at the bank. Not people of great sophistication or great intellectually based people, but they surprise you. They'll come up with a pretty good verdict. Most of the time they come up with a better answer than we think they will."

One such case was an eminent domain case on Cumberland Island, Georgia, where his client was James Stillman Rockefeller, president of National City Bank, now Citigroup. There was talk of having the case tried elsewhere on the premise that a jury in south Georgia wouldn't give a Rockefeller a fair case. "I had a real problem with that. The Rockefellers are entitled to be treated just as fairly as the poorest individual in Brunswick. And that's where the case was going to be tried. We tried the case. They had five appraisers. I had one. My appraiser said it was worth six-and-a-half million dollars and their appraisers said it was worth about six hundred thousand dollars. The jury went out on Thanksgiving Day and said the property was worth six-and-a-half million dollars. And I thought it was interesting because my whole argument was predicated upon the fact that a Rockefeller is entitled to the same breath of fresh air as a Cook or a Smith or a Jones. If it's not that way, somebody is miserably misled. And the jury rose to that occasion. The foreman of the jury was a truck driver."

Mr. Cook has also become adept at reading his clients, especially when they may not be telling him the truth. "If I'm not quite sure, sometimes I'm pretty damn sure, well then I might say to the guy, 'Look, now surely you don't expect me to believe that, do you?' Because as I have often said to the clients, you might fool me, but I'm not the one that you need to fool. You need to tell me the truth so I can deal with your problem and put it in the right perspective. I think I have a pretty good way of dealing with people, and in an overwhelming number of cases, I think I am able to get at the truth. The client makes a terrible mistake if he misleads the lawyer because it usually crops up at the worst time. The worst thing in the world that can happen to you, and I've had this happen, is get into the courtroom and you've got a witness on the stand and you're hearing things that you've never heard before from your client. And I look over at the client, and he said, 'Maybe I'd better tell you about this.' Well, he should have told me about it six months ago in the office, and he wouldn't have had that problem."

Mr. Cook has also fired clients, one just recently. "He wanted me to do something that I couldn't do, that would have violated ethical constraints. I gave him his file, and I told him I was sure he would probably be able to find somebody that would do it, but it wouldn't be me."

Obviously things have changed since the days when you could hang your shingle out from your office over the drugstore and expect to get cases. So for young lawyers who are starting their practice, Mr. Cook advises them to take every opportunity to speak, whether it's at the Rotary Club, the Lion's Club, the local high school or the local junior college. "There are many ways of getting known and telling people that you're a pretty smart young lawyer," he said.

The one thing he is adamantly opposed to: blatant advertising. "I am appalled when I look in the Yellow Pages and I see a lawyer with a full-page ad. And he does everything. He's been practicing about three years maybe and he or she is an expert in every field. I understand the rationale of the Supreme Court ruling authorizing such advertising, it being pro-consumerism. But I find the whole concept of advertising as we see it today as a terrible way of getting business. I've often said that in the first twenty years of my law practice I got more calls from my creditors than I did from my clients. But you've just got to be patient with it."

Mr. Cook has practiced law so long, he's represented four generations of the same family. "As old as I am, I've outlived most of my detractors," he said with a chuckle.

He believes a great lawyer, no matter what type he is, has to be dedicated to what he is doing. "He's got to believe that what he does in the law practice is the right thing to do and that's he's making a contribution, not only from the standpoint of making a living, but that's he's making a contribution to the institution of law. If a lawyer or a doctor got into his profession because he thought he was going to get rich – if that was the deciding factor, then he's made a hell of a mistake. If a lawyer believes as I believe, if he looks after his clients, if he is

# The one thing he is adamantly opposed to: blatant advertising.

loyal to his clients and he applies himself assiduously and with deliberation to what he does, he'll make all the money that he needs. And sometimes he'll be lucky as hell and he'll make more than he needs."

# Summary

- Be civil with clients. "You've got to be understanding of their problems. You deal with people who are sophisticated, you deal with uneducated people, you deal with people who are less understanding than others. But you've got to listen. And if you learn to listen, you'll learn a lot."

- Return phone calls. "I always return all of my calls. I get calls from people I don't know, and for half of them there's nothing I can do. But I talk to them. I'm civil with them. Returning calls is a very important thing in the law practice. You never can get too big for your britches."

- Be truthful with your client. "It's essential, overwhelmingly essential, for lawyers to be absolutely, totally, critically honest with their clients. Everybody wants to hear good news. You cannot just tell your client what he or she wants to hear. We want to be optimistic but you can't give good news all the time."

- Have a good work ethic and follow a timetable. "Some of us tend to be a little lazy. Good lawyers, successful lawyers, have a dedicated work ethic and have a timetable for everything. And you've got to keep your eye on what you're doing and look after your business in a timely fashion."

- Believe in what you're doing. "You've got to have a well-settled belief that what you're doing is a little more than just making a living. You've got to feel like you're making some contribution – for institutional change."

- Take every opportunity to speak to groups. "There are many ways of getting known and telling people that you're a pretty smart young lawyer."

# Bobby Lee Cook

Bobby Lee Cook attended college at Vanderbilt University and the University of Alabama. He went to law school at Vanderbilt, but took the bar early, passed it, and started his own law practice. He is a partner in the Summerville, Georgia, firm of Cook & Connelly, and served one term in the Georgia House of Representatives, one term in the Georgia Senate, and four years as a trial judge. He is a founding member of the Roscoe Pound Foundation and the Trial Lawyers for Public Justice, and he is a past chair of the Board of Regents of the National College of Criminal Defense Lawyers. Mr. Cook is a fellow of the American College of Trial Lawyers and the American Board of Criminal Lawyers and is a member of the International Society of Barristers.

Mr. Cook has been honored by the American Academy of Achievement, was the first recipient of the Georgia Bar Tradition of Excellence Award, received the California Attorneys for Criminal Justice annual award, and in 1994 was selected as Trial Lawyer of the Year at the Georgia Bar annual meeting. The ABA Journal has noted that the Matlock television series was based on him and his career as a criminal defense lawyer.

# Clay Long

Partner
McKenna Long & Aldridge

I t's all about relationships. That about sums up Clay Long's philosophy of the practice of law. Having good, personal relationships with clients, with people in your firm, and with the people you deal with outside the firm is absolutely indispensable in the practice of law.

"Nobody likes to have a lawyer," he said. "So you want them to say, if I have to have a lawyer, this is the one I want because I really like him and I trust him and he's going to do what he says he's going to do. A client can tell if you are doing what he wants you to do – delivering on time, being there when he needs you, dropping everything and going to take care of a big problem."

Mr. Long believes you also must have good relationships with the people you practice law with because you will always need help. And you need to have a good relationship with people outside of your firm so that they trust you when you deal with them.

"You've got a problem and you've got to get somebody else in your firm to drop what they're doing and help you out. Or you need three young associates to help you and they decide whom they want to work for. Outside of the firm, you're dealing with other people all the time, whether it's judges or people on the other side of transactions or lenders. You have to have a reputation so that you can go and meet with a government official and tell him what's going on and he believes it because he knows you wouldn't tell him that if it weren't true."

Mr. Long has built numerous relationships in his long career. He is a founding partner and former co-chairman of McKenna Long & Aldridge. He started Long Aldridge & Norman in 1974 with just three other attorneys and it quickly became one of the fastest growing law firms in the Southeast. In 2002, the firm merged with Washington DC-based McKenna & Cuneo, and now has 450 attorneys in ten U.S. cities and Brussels, Belgium. Mr. Long stepped down as chairman in 2005 after leading the firm for thirty-one years and returned to practicing law full time.

He hadn't really planned on being a lawyer. After he lost his parents at a young age while growing up in Demopolis, Alabama, he lived with the family of a Methodist minister for a year. He entered Birmingham-Southern College planning to become a Methodist minister himself. But as he said, he never does things the easy way or ends up doing what he meant to do.

## Mr. Long learned a valuable lesson about relationships during his effort to get his first job: be respectful of everyone you meet.

"As the Methodists would say, I fell from grace. I was an English major and I thought maybe I'd be an English professor. But it didn't take me long to figure out that was a good way to starve. I was interested in communication, language, the written word, the spoken word, also every now and then listening. So law seemed like a good thing for me to gravitate to."

After he graduated in 1958 he was awarded a scholarship to attend the University of London for a year. There he met his wife Elizabeth, who is from California and was studying in London as well. They married and moved to Cambridge, Massachusetts, where Mr. Long attended Harvard Law School. (After their two daughters were in school, his wife went to law school at Emory University. She is a Fulton County Superior Court judge.)

Mr. Long learned a valuable lesson about relationships during his effort to get his first job: be respectful of everyone you meet.

He wanted to clerk for Justice Hugo Black, an Alabaman who was appointed to the United States Supreme Court in 1937. Mr. Long learned that Justice Black had never hired a person he hadn't met, but he didn't grant interviews.

"So that was a little conundrum. How was I going to get this worked out? I called his office and told his secretary, a woman named Frances Lamb, that I was going to be in Washington on Friday and asked if I could just come by and say hello to the judge. She said that Friday is the conference day, on which all the judges meet to decide the cases that have been argued that week. Sometimes they're not finished until eight o'clock p.m. and sometimes they're out and gone by three o'clock. But she said, 'If you want to come over here and sit, I'll see if I can get you in, but I can't promise.' So I went over and sat in the office with her all day, until about eight o'clock, when he came shuffling in. She got me in to see him, and I saw him for probably about thirty seconds, and he went home because he was older and he was tired. But I had spent the day with Frances, who was a very close confidante of his and a very good secretary. I found out later that every time that he would say, 'Now, let me see the résumés, I need to think about a clerk,' she would take mine out and put it on top."

Although Mr. Long modestly attributes his hiring over the many other qualified people to luck, most would view it as a lesson in persistence and the value of building a relationship with the judge's secretary.

After clerking for a year, Mr. Long moved to Atlanta where he went to work for Sutherland Asbill & Brennan. The firm had around fifteen to twenty lawyers at the time, and was primarily known as a tax firm. Not really wanting to be a tax lawyer, he

*In 2000 Governor Roy Barnes swears in members of the Georgia Greenspace Commission, of which Clay Long served as chairman.*

accepted a job under the conditions that he not do any tax work, and if it didn't work out in Atlanta, he could move to the Washington office.

"The first week I was there, Randolph Thrower, who was a senior tax partner, came in and said, 'I have this little case I want you to help me with.' I worked on it for a year. It was a tax case. I did a lot of tax work for a while and corporate work and other things. You have to roll with the punches. I was at a really wonderful firm and it was a chance to work with Randolph, one of the great lawyers in Atlanta. So I didn't care."

From there he transitioned to doing real estate work, as those transactions involved a lot of tax work. Mr. Long worked with a developer named Barney Wiggins, and a few years later he asked Mr. Long to join his real estate company.

"I was with him for two years and it was a lot of fun. Barney was a great partner, but in that period of time I realized I was really a lawyer. I wasn't a businessman. I wanted to do legal work. John Aldridge was my lawyer then and we started talking about working together. He had just been offered a partnership at Sutherland, and he said, 'If I accept the offer I want it to be for life, so now is the time we better talk about it.' So we decided with two other lawyers, Bill Stevens and Bill Summer, to form this firm in 1974. It wasn't something I meant to do. That's a pattern you may see in my life. But it's been great fun."

Back then the legal community was less mobile and people didn't often leave a law firm to start another firm. But while working with Mr. Wiggins in a small organization, Mr. Long became used to doing things the way he wanted to. "I was ready to have at it and do it my way. And John felt the same way. Our plan was to work hard and have a good time and respond to every opportunity that came along. We were much more focused on this year and next year and not where this would end up."

The firm grew fairly quickly, with Barney Wiggins as one of the first clients. Mr. Long employed other ways to get clients – he asked for the work through relationships he had and started out with small legal matters.

*Clay Long receives an Honorary Doctor of Laws degree from Birmingham-Southern College in 2002.*

He had done work for the Ford Foundation, which had a lot of investments in Atlanta, when he was at Sutherland. Mr. Long went to New York to visit his friend and Harvard Law School classmate, Bevis Longstreth, who was their principal outside lawyer and told him his firm would like to work for the Foundation. Mr. Longstreth went to the person in charge of real estate investment at the Ford Foundation and said he wanted to use Mr. Long's firm.

"This guy looked at him and said, 'The Ford Foundation has never used a four-person firm.' And Mr. Longstreth said, 'I will vouch for them.' And the Ford Foundation hired us. Thanks to John Aldridge, we were also doing just a small amount of work for what was then First Atlanta and now Wachovia. But as a result of these engagements, we were appearing in transactions in which you wouldn't normally expect to see a firm that young and that small."

Mr. Long believes he benefited a lot from referrals from classmates at Harvard Law School. "I think that is primarily because the classes were big, around 500 people. They were large classes as law schools go, and they're capable people who were ambitious and worked hard, and they ended up in a lot of big cities and big firms. It was less something that I did consciously and more just the good fortune of having been in a place you were fortunate to be."

Although Atlanta suffered a downturn in the real estate market in the mid seventies, that dip actually presented an opportunity for the young law firm.

"Prior to that time, law firms had not been all that careful about conflicts of interest. It was very common for a firm to represent a developer and also represent the bank. The firm would just close the loan, representing the transaction. Nobody thought about it much during those booming times. But when the market went sour, and the lender wanted to be paid and the borrower couldn't pay, well, then you had a real conflict, and the firms couldn't represent both of them in those cases. Firms had to send at least one of them, and in some cases both, to another firm. We always got a lot of that conflict work. I believe it was because we were good enough to do the work, but these firms felt that we were so small that we couldn't possibly steal their clients. And we never did. We never tried. That was part of the deal. But this turmoil in the legal community as well as the real estate community was a big boost to us in the early days."

Mr. Long believes in a small, growing firm you have to deal with two slightly separate issues. One, how do you build your own practice; the other, how do you attract clients?

"The number one thing is hard work. I've never seen anything worthwhile that you wanted to do that didn't require a lot of hard work. Certainly in the legal profession I have never seen a great lawyer who didn't work hard. I've seen a lot of people who started off kind of mediocre but they kept working and they kept growing and they got better and better. I've seen a lot of success with people who you might not have predicted would be that successful. This is not a business where you take a big risk and get a big hit and isn't that great. It's a daily service business. You get up in the morning, you do what you have to do, your clients call you, you respond to that, and that's what it's about."

In addition to building his practice, Mr. Long also had to lead a growing law firm.

"I used to say my style of leadership is that I find out wherever the crowd is gathering and run over there and get in front of it. Because I think there's a lot of truth in that. If you want your organization to be successful, you have to understand the goals and ambitions and desires of your most productive people. And those have to become the values and the goals and objectives of your law firm. Because if they're not aligned, then you lose too many key people. If they are aligned, you're got a strong, vibrant organization, and other people can be supportive of that and do extremely well and make a lot of money and be great lawyers. But the most productive people have got to share values with the institution that you're creating or it doesn't work."

> # McKenna Long & Aldridge is recognized as having the first and largest government contracts practice in the United States.

Another area of practice in which his firm became involved was government relations, which started for Long & Aldridge when the firm was very small and was asked to work in the cable television industry. Now, thanks to the McKenna Cuneo merger, McKenna Long & Aldridge has become recognized for having the first and largest government contracts practice in the United States.

"It's part of this service we deliver. If somebody has a government contract and they have overruns, we can help them with that. If somebody's looking to get a contract awarded, we know who's awarding it, and how the process works, and how you respond to requests for proposals and all that kind of stuff. And if you get in trouble, that's one of the things that lawyers do, too. It's a part of the whole package."

Mr. Long met a lot of people in the early days of the firm's government work, including Michael Lomax, who was then chairman of the Fulton County Commission. Mr. Lomax put Mr. Long on the board of MARTA, Atlanta's public transportation system, where Mr. Long became very involved and served as chairman.

At that time his firm was fairly young, and Mr. Long worked long hours. "I spent about fifty percent of my time on MARTA business, fifty percent of my time on the firm's business, and about fifty percent of my time on clients' business. And that's what it was like. It was wild. It wasn't going to last long, just a couple of years. It was a price worth paying."

Devoting that much time to an outside organization wasn't the most popular thing he did at the firm. "But it seemed to me that it was such a unique opportunity and such a special opportunity for me at a young age that it was something I needed to do. And everybody supported that. And there's no question that I was more visible as a result of that kind of effort."

That was the beginning of Mr. Long's interest in conservation, livable communities, green space and clean air. "MARTA was a great eye-opener to me because it involved looking at urban problems and urban livability and transportation and how you move people around and how you have an environment like this that works." Mr. Long also served as chairman of the Georgia Conservancy and Georgia Greenspace Commission, in addition to his work with several other community organizations.

"All of that involved politics and it just became increasingly important to me. If you think about it, clients sometimes want the government to do something for them, like give them a franchise or give them a license. Sometimes they want to do something for the government. They want a government contract to build airplanes or whatever. And sometimes they want to stop the government from doing something to them because they got in some kind of regulatory trouble. So much of what they do has to do with the government. So if you're their advisor, their counselor, their warrior, you've got to build a deal with the government. And the more you get involved in that, it sort of feeds on itself."

Although he met a lot of people through this type of work, he said you never get anything done just because you know somebody. "What you get is your phone call returned because they know you're an honorable, straight person and you're a friend, and you'll call them and they'll listen to you. You still have to be right. But you have to be able to facilitate. So, I think we were the first people in Atlanta that identified it as a critical piece of practicing law and built a unit to do that. And I know we were the first firm to hire non-lawyers to work in that group under the supervision of lawyers."

## "I believe that you build your practice with these personal relationships and people come to you because they have met you and they like you."

Mr. Long's advice to young attorneys is to first do a good job for the partner you are working for. "You're only marginally related to the client, anyway. But if you do a good job for that partner and that client two or three times, and then that partner is busy doing something else, and he says to you, 'Will you call Joe? I'm busy.' So the young lawyer calls him and all of a sudden Joe figures out he can get it done faster and cheaper with this young guy and he's happy about that."

And that, said Mr. Long, is where young lawyers can make a mistake. "They think they're just doing the legal work and that it's just about providing that service. Well, it is about providing that service. That's the base. But if you don't try to learn more about the people with whom you work, what they care about and what their passions are, you're missing out because everybody's out there soliciting business. People are working your clients all the time. If you're not paying attention to them and caring about them and knowing how they think, what they feel, eventually they're going to dry up. We've all had that happen. You have a good client, and you get busy doing something else, and a year goes by and you look back and wonder, what happened to Fred?"

Mr. Long acknowledges that the pressure for billable hours is more of an issue now that it was in the past. "I know that I and many others worked just as hard as people work today but it wasn't so focused on the billable hours. We spent more time doing other things. I think the really good young lawyers are still doing that. They're still out there talking to people and getting to know them, watching their friends and seeing who's moving up in their organizations.

"I believe that you build your practice with these personal relationships and people come to you because they have met you and they like you. You're out in the community and they've seen that you're a responsible person. Their best friend recommends you. I consider it more just personal development and personal relationships. I'm not big on marketing in the sense that it's used today. I acknowledge that you've got to get legal work in some way. But there's a tone about it that I think professionals should maintain and they should do it in an honorable and reasonable way. Some of the young lawyers I see now are doing it all right. They're meeting this challenge in a spectacular way."

*Clay Long with Governor Sonny Perdue as he announced the Georgia Land Conservation Partnership Plan, designed by Mr. Long and his Blue Ribbon Committee in August 2004.*

Although devoting his time and talents to outside organizations was rewarding and did bring business to his law firm, Mr. Long doesn't advocate those activities solely for the purpose of bringing in business.

"I would think it's a relatively inefficient way to do it. You put in so much time for the benefit. On the other hand, there's absolutely no doubt that Atlanta is a city that has been built on merit. This city has always opened up its arms to new people who come in and pay their dues. And I think that's a great spirit for a city. If you come here like I did with no family ties and very few contacts and you have the good things happen to you that have happened to me, and you don't feel some obligation to give back, there's something wrong with you. And so I've always believed that that's part of who you need to be. And that really isn't unique to lawyering or anything else. If you're part of a community and you're blessed with so many of the material and psychic rewards that a community can give you, then you need to be giving something back."

Mr. Long's advice to young lawyers on building a reputation is to start with people in their own firm. "I think they volunteer to participate in the building of a house for

Habitat and they show up on a Saturday with their hammer and nails. They're watching each other all the time. You can't really fool anybody. I think you have to care so you have to pick things that you want to do. When my girls were little, and I was working a lot, way too much I'm sure, at one point Elizabeth was talking to me about spending more time with the girls. One of the things I liked to do in those days was to ride a bicycle a lot. It occurred to me that a good thing to do with my children was something I wanted to do anyway. So we'd go bike riding together. I think the same thing is true, how will I build a reputation? You do it by doing things that you want to do that you are committed to, that you care about, and then it's pretty much natural."

And being reliable is a virtue that tops his list. "If I ask my assistant to mail this check off today because it's got to go today, and she says I'll take care of it, I'll never have to think about it again. But if I come in tomorrow and it's sitting on her desk, that's not good. You're much better off saying, 'I can't do that, sorry, I don't have the time; I don't have that skill,' whatever it is. You shouldn't be taking on things you can't handle."

*With Attorney General Thurbert Baker in 2005. Clay Long serves as special assistant attorney general for tri-state water litigation involving Georgia, Alabama, and Florida.*

One of the things he enjoys about the legal profession is that people are on hand who can help you. "You can have a lot of flexibility in the way you practice. As a friend of mine said once, 'It's all about intake.' Once you've committed, then you've got to do everything you can do, because you've committed to that. So you just commit less. That's about the front end of the process."

In addition to providing legal services, Mr. Long believes law firms have an obligation to provide training to young associates. "I've always believed that every lawyer here should be loyal to us, should be dedicated to us, and we should be loyal to them and be dedicated to them, but I want them to have the basic skills so that if they weren't happy here, or we weren't happy with them, they're going to be all right.

"I remember one time one of our associates who was about a year from being a partner said that she wanted to concentrate in a certain area. She came to talk to me about it, and I asked her why she wanted to do that, and she said that one of the partners here had asked her to do that. I told her that's fine if that's what you want to do. But if that doesn't work out, you won't be made a partner. It's your life. You need to make sure that that's what you want to do and that's what you think will work for you.

As far as specializing, Mr. Long doesn't believe it is either a good thing or a bad thing.

"I think it depends on the person you're talking about. The best specialists are absolute experts in some areas of the law, maybe subject matter, maybe an industry, but they clearly work on understanding the context in which their issues arise. The good ones are more than just specialists. They're part of the team that's getting that job done and they know what that job is. But you know there's so much law now, it's hard. If you take the benefits, the risk area, the tax area, securities law, intellectual property, it's tough. It's harder than it was. I respect these kids for wanting to be able to do something well."

> "You're going to be under a lot of stress because everything we do involves a problem."

Mr. Long said it is regularly alleged that there are a lot of people practicing law who are not happy. His advice to them? Quit.

"I don't believe that this is something you should do if you don't really love it, if you don't really feel good about it. It's a service business. Somebody may decide to call you at two o'clock in the morning, but they're in charge. You're a helper. You're an enabler. You can make it happen with them and sometimes for them. But it's not your show. I'm just a hired gun. Tell me what you want me to do and I'll do it for you, or I'll figure out how you can do it. So a lawyer has to get comfortable with that."

He also believes young attorneys have to be willing to work hard and handle a certain amount of stress. "You're going to be under a lot of stress because everything we do involves a problem. It's either a big problem because somebody sued your client for ten million dollars or it's a little problem because your client wants to close that deal, or whatever. The real training of lawyers is to solve problems. If you ever watch a couple of businessmen try to work out a deal, and a couple of lawyers working on the same deal, the business guys are trying to say, 'No, that's not a problem. Oh, we can solve that.' The lawyers say, 'How are we going to solve that problem?' The businessman's job is to get it done and not rock the boat and keep everybody happy and on the same page, and our job is make sure it doesn't bite you two years later. It's just a different training and a different mindset. It probably takes both to get where you want to be, but again, if you're not happy forcing the issue – what are we going to do about x? What if x happens? If you don't like that role, you need to get out of this business.

"I think it's a hard life. It's a very rewarding life and I love it, but it's not a game. Every now and then we have associates who, maybe they've come from a good family with a fair amount of material success, and they go to college and they go to law school and they come to work, and it's like a game. They haven't really figured out that this is real money and real people and real decisions are being made and lives are being built or ruined. And that puts a lot of stress on you if you really care. And if you don't care, it's a bad business. I think if you do really care, this stuff gets a lot easier. You make choices and you pay the price of those choices. But you need to be happy with the price."

# Summary

• Good relationships with clients, relationships with people in your firm and relationships with the people you deal with outside the firm are absolutely indispensable in the practice of law. "You have to have good, personal relationships with a lot of people. Obviously you've got to have that with your clients. Start with people in your own firm."

• Be respectful of everyone you meet. Mr. Long was awarded a clerkship with a Supreme Court Judge after spending the day with his secretary while waiting to meet the judge.

• Roll with the punches. Mr. Long joined a law firm known as a tax firm under the condition that he not do any tax work. "The first week I was there, Randolph Thrower, who was a senior tax partner, came in and said, 'I have this little case I want you to help me with.' I worked on it for a year. It was a tax case. I was at a really wonderful firm and it was a chance to work with him. He's one of the great lawyers in Atlanta. So I didn't care."

• Ask for work from people you know. If necessary, start out with small legal matters. After asking for work through a Harvard Law School classmate, Mr. Long's firm was hired by the Ford Foundation. "We were also doing just a small amount of work for what was then First Atlanta, now Wachovia. But as a result of that, we were appearing in transactions in which you wouldn't normally expect to see a firm that young and that small."

• The number one thing is hard work. "I've never seen anything worthwhile that you wanted to do that didn't require a lot of hard work. Certainly in the legal profession I have never seen a great lawyer who didn't work hard."

• The practice of law is a daily service business. "You get up in the morning, you do what you have to do, your clients call you, you respond to that, and that's what it's about."

• Dealing with clients is not just about providing a service. "If you don't try to learn more about the people with whom you work, what they care about and what their passions are, you're missing out because everybody's out there soliciting business. People are working your clients all the time. So if you're not paying attention to them and caring about them and knowing how they think, what they feel, eventually they're going to dry up."

• Do a good job for the partner you are working for. "You're only marginally related to the client, anyway. But you do a good job for that partner and that client two or three times, and then that partner is busy doing something else, and he says to you, 'Will you call Joe? I'm busy.' So your lawyer calls him and all of a sudden Joe figures out he can get it done faster and cheaper with this young guy and he's happy about that."

• Be reliable. Commit to do what you say you will and don't take on things you can't handle.

• Get comfortable with the fact that it's not your show. "You're a helper. You're an enabler. I'm just a hired gun. Tell me what you want me to do and I'll do it for you, or I'll figure out how you can do it."

# Clay Long

Clay Long is a founding partner and former co-chairman of McKenna Long & Aldridge.

Mr. Long's practice focuses on general business and corporate matters, with a concentration in the purchase, sale and merger of businesses, and real estate development and finance. He has represented companies in the food and beverage business such as Coca-Cola Enterprises, The Krystal Company, and President Baking Company; in the communications industry such as Cablecasting, Ltd., Cable America, CableSouth and World Access; merchant banks and venture capital firms, such as First Capital Management and Alliance Technology Ventures and agriservices, such as Monsanto. In the real estate area, Mr. Long currently represents, among others, Corporate Holdings, Inc., the real estate holding company of John Williams, and all of the Williams-related funds. For the last several years, Mr. Long has represented the State of Georgia in the Tri-State water wars.

Mr. Long is also active in alternative dispute resolution. He regularly acts as an arbitrator or mediator in complex corporate and real estate disputes, construction disputes, and matters involving valuation, tax, accounting, and financing issues. He recently finished his term as President of the Georgia Arbitrators Forum.

Mr. Long's passion for many years has been the environment and conservation. He has served as chairman of the board of MARTA, which focused on the adverse environmental impacts of sprawl, including gridlock and air pollution. Mr. Long has also served as chairman of the Georgia Conservancy, where he helped develop its influential smart growth program called "Blueprints for Successful Living."

Mr. Long chaired an advisory committee appointed by former Governor Roy Barnes to recommend a program to protect community greenspace. Mr. Long then chaired the Georgia Greenspace Commission, which supervised the granting of more than sixty million dollars to local governments for the acquisition of greenspace. Then in January 2004, Governor Perdue appointed Mr. Long to chair his advisory council for the Georgia Land Conservation Partnership. The Council proposed a statewide, comprehensive land conservation plan. The recommendations of the Council were included in the Georgia Land Conservation Act, which was passed in early 2005.

In addition to his conservation activities, Mr. Long has served as president of the Atlanta United Way and has been a member of the board of directors of Research Atlanta, the Atlanta Urban League, Birmingham-Southern College, the Atlanta-Fulton County Public Library, the Metropolitan Atlanta Community Foundation, the Georgia Department of Community Affairs, and the Atlanta Rotary Club. In addition, Mr. Long has been president of the Harvard Law School Association of Georgia, a participant in Leadership Atlanta and an adjunct professor of law on mergers and acquisitions at Georgia State University College of Law.

In 1989, Mr. Long was the first recipient of the Atlanta Bar Association's Leadership Award. In 2002, he received an honorary Doctor of Laws degree from Birmingham-Southern College, having earlier been given its Distinguished Alumni Award. In 2004, he received the Lifetime Achievement Award from the Anti-Defamation League, the Volunteer of the Year Award from the Georgia Environmental Council, and the Public Service Award from the Georgia Parks and Recreation Authority. In 2005, Mr. Long was *honored by the Georgian Wildlife Foundation as the "Conservationist of the Year" and by the Georgia Conservancy with its "Distinguished Conservationist" Award. In 2008, Mr. Long received the prestigious Armin Maier Award from the Rotary Club of Atlanta for his years of active community service.*

*For many years, Mr. Long has been included in* Georgia Trend Magazine's *"100 Most Influential Georgians" and in lists of top lawyers in the U.S. and in Georgia. In 2005, 2006 and 2007, he was designated one of "Georgia's Most Influential People" by* James Magazine. *He has also been listed in* The Best Lawyers in America *for over 20 years.*

# Frank Love Jr.

Retired Partner
Powell Goldstein*
Former Chair, Litigation Department

When Frank Love Jr. joined the law firm of Powell Goldstein in 1951, the ink on his diploma from Washington and Lee University was barely dry. He earned his law degree there in 1951, after receiving his undergraduate diploma in 1950.

A native of Fayetteville, West Virginia, Mr. Love said he was placed at Washington and Lee by his father, also a graduate.

"I was discharged from the Navy in August and had asked him to please get me into a coed school, preferably Duke, which was where I really wanted to go. However, when I got out, I was enrolled in Washington and Lee and had to start a week later. He told me that was the only school he could have me admitted to. Years later, I found all my other applications, including the one for Duke. He had never sent them in!"

Back then the firm was known as Powell, Goldstein, Frazer & Murphy. The name reduction came in 2004, following the trend towards shorter law firm names for branding and marketing purposes. Of course, many lawyers refer to it by its even shorter name: "Pogo." With the addition of Mr. Love in 1951, the firm had eight lawyers.

Although Mr. Love had offers from other firms during his career, he always made the decision to stay. After retiring from the firm in 1998, he maintains an office at Powell Goldstein and goes in three days a week. "I play golf three days a week, and the other day I have to work on my honey-do list," he jokes.

Founded in 1909, Powell Goldstein now has more than 300 lawyers in Atlanta, Washington, D.C., Dallas, Texas and Charlotte, North Carolina. But the firms' lawyers weren't always fond of adding lawyers to the firm.

Mr. Love recalls when he was first hired that fall of 1951. "There was a reluctance to expand back then. The firm didn't hire anyone unless they had to, absolutely *had* to.

---

* On January 1, 2009 Powell Goldstein merged with Bryan Cave. The Atlanta office is doing business under the name of Bryan Cave Powell Goldstein.

I was lucky to get a job. But the partners were not all that convinced that I was going to be a trial lawyer," said the man who ended up being the chairman of the litigation department. "When I started work here, of course there was very little specialization. You did everything: real estate, divorces, adoptions, or whatever. But the primary source of business at that time in this firm was litigation, so everybody did litigation. Buck Murphy, even later our top corporate lawyers like Elliot Goldstein tried cases. Associates were trained by helping partners try cases.

"I went with Ed Dorsey or Buck Murphy and carried their briefcases, and they might ask me to examine a witness or whatever. I would not do a whole lot except pay attention to what was going on."

But then he got his big chance, in a case that he recalls as his most memorable case. "Ed Dorsey gave me a case called *Byars v. Associated Cab Company*. It was a plaintiff's case, and it had been sitting around the firm for years because nobody thought it was winnable. So when Ed gave it to me, he thought, well, let's give him some experience. Whoever tries it is going to lose it, anyhow. And I tried it and won it. And that amazed everybody. And that helped a lot."

So they gave him another difficult case, *Miller vs. Wilensky Leather Company*. "I got a verdict I was told was the biggest verdict ever rendered in Fulton Superior Court in a back injury case. Of course, that was fifty years ago, and wouldn't be a big deal today but back then, it was such a big verdict that the firm closed and we all went to Herron's Restaurant and had a martini. From then on I didn't have any trouble getting cases referred to me within the firm. I had pretty good security from then on."

Another way Mr. Love built his practice was from becoming known in his neighborhood. Shortly after he married his wife Libby in 1952, they moved to Sandy Springs.

"They were condemning everybody's land out there, widening Roswell Road, building I-285, building I-75 and so forth. The people there knew I was a lawyer, so I started getting their condemnation cases. And that practice just grew and grew. That's a circumstance where you don't have one client who sends you lots of business, but several clients that send you some business. And then after I had handled who knows how many such cases, the firm recognized that I had become a specialist in that area and started sending me cases that came in that involved eminent domain."

Mr. Love enjoyed trying those cases and had a substantial inventory of eminent domain cases during most of the years he practiced.

Other clients Mr. Love has represented over the years include one of the nation's largest broadcast and publishing companies, a major producer of gypsum, a major automotive parts manufacturer, and a national veterans organization.

One of his biggest clients from a standpoint of volume and longevity was insurance giant State Farm. The firm was already representing State Farm and dealing with a huge inventory of cases when Mr. Love was employed. Until the firm phased out of doing insurance defense work, Mr. Love had a large volume of these cases from all over metropolitan Atlanta. In one memorable year, he tried every civil case heard in Gwinnett County, most of them State Farm cases.

> "When I started work here, of course there was very little specialization. You did everything: real estate, divorces, adoptions."

For a long time, he also represented Travers Insurance Agency, a client that he generated himself – although not in quite the way he could have imagined.

"A friend of mine was an agent for Travers, and he kept bugging me to get an interview with the people who were handling our insurance program so he could try to sell them a policy with Travers," he said. "I finally succeeded in doing that, and I told him that I expected some help in exchange. He kept bugging the people at Travers to send me some business, and I finally got one case. I later learned that that was the only case I was ever going to get through him."

But that's not the end of the story. "I tried that case in Warren County and the foreman of that jury called the claims manager at Travers. He told him that he was insured by Travers and he was gratified to know that if he ever had an accident, he would be defended by good counsel.

"I was president of the Georgia Defense Lawyers Association at that time, and about a week later we had an event and the claims manager was a speaker on my program. We were socializing, and I told him that I had just tried a case for him, and that it had turned out quite well. He said, 'Oh, you're the guy that juror called me about.' I didn't know of course that the juror had called him. That was news to me. From then on, I got a huge volume of cases from Travers."

Mr. Love got another big client because a friend of his became president of a company that owned hospitals for alcoholics and people with other substance abuse problems.

"It was national in scope, and I represented them for a number of years. At one time I had twenty-two lawyers in the firm working for that client. After my friend resigned, I continued to represent them until the company was purchased and moved to California."

Mobil Oil was one of Mr. Love's big clients for several years. "I represented Mobil Oil for as long as they were in Georgia, probably around ten years. We handled their litigation, real estate transactions and other matters. They moved into the state and opened eighty-some stations, but later closed them and moved out. We still had a lot of lease disputes et cetera, to handle."

*Frank Love Jr. in his Midtown Atlanta office, where he still goes to work three days a week.*

Mobil Oil became a client through the case of an unfortunate man who lost his thumb. Twice.

"One of my partners, who practiced in wills, estates, and trusts, had a classmate who was with Mobil. And Mobil Chemical Company was building a plant somewhere in the metro area. They had a worker's comp claim, rather a weird one, by a man who lost the same thumb, twice. He lost his thumb in an accident, and then lost his surgically replaced thumb in another accident.

"He called my partner, who didn't know a thing about workman's comp, so he sent the case to me and I handled it. And about a year later, they had a serious claim, and the only lawyer whose name they had was mine. Steve Mulliken, who later became a very close friend of mine, called me to see if I would look at it and I did. He said, 'We can't win this but we've got to do something with it.' I said, 'I think I can win it.' And I did. I went on to handle a substantial inventory of cases for them."

Another client Mr. Love represented was Seaboard Surety Company, which at one time insured most of the media in Atlanta. He earned the company as a client although his experience with this area of the law was rather limited.

"I had just tried a plaintiff's case for libel and slander and won a nice verdict. One of my partners, who is no longer with us, was having lunch with one of the Seaboard Surety people. The Seaboard person told him that they were looking for a lawyer to handle their libel and slander claims. My partner said, 'Oh yeah, one of my partners just got a big verdict. He knows all about libel and slander.' I really didn't because it was the only such case I had ever handled. But I learned a lot. At least enough."

So Seaboard Surety hired Mr. Love. He won that first case they sent him and several others in succession. He represented the company until it left the Atlanta market.

> "My partner said, 'Oh yeah, one of my partners just got a big verdict. He knows all about libel and slander.' I really didn't because it was the only case I had ever had. But I learned a lot."

Although he enjoyed working with most all of his clients, Mr. Love remembers one that was probably the most fun. The Carolina Cougars was a professional basketball team that was the first to use the regional concept, dividing its time between Greensboro, Charlotte, and Raleigh, North Carolina. Members of the American Basketball Association, the team lasted from 1969 to 1974.

Mr. Love won that business because a client of the firm bought the team. Although Mr. Love had not done any work for him, they had become friends, had played golf together and the client knew Mr. Love was a basketball fan. While representing the Cougars, he was involved in several cases of "recruiting" players from other professional basketball teams.

"I was very successful and so became general counsel. We signed Joe Caldwell from the Atlanta Hawks, and we won that case. Billy Cunningham was signed from the Philadelphia 76ers. We won that case, as well. We also recruited a seven foot, two-inch ballplayer named Jim McDaniels, and at one time we had seven cases pending in five states over that little transaction, which fortunately was eventually settled."

One of the reasons Mr. Love enjoyed working with the Carolina Cougars so much was the people with whom he worked. "I was crazy about Tedd Munchack [who purchased the Cougar franchise in 1970]. I also really liked Billy Cunningham and Joe Caldwell. In most matters I was involved in representing the Cougars or the old ABA and the lawyers involved were always the same. Like a little 'club.' We got to know each other and enjoyed fighting all day and having a good time at night. I was particularly close to Bynum Hunter from North Carolina who was on the other side of every litigated basketball case I handled. In addition the people involved in basketball were an interesting bunch. Owners' meetings were a hoot."

Although specialization is now accepted in the business and legal communities, that wasn't always the case. Not all clients were happy about the change, and sometimes it was a problem.

"I had a client named Bill Marrett, who was a golf buddy of mine. He owned two or three companies, and he had always had one lawyer who handled all of his legal business. He was convinced that that's what you needed – one lawyer to handle all of his legal needs. Then one day he told me, 'My lawyer has gotten too old and can't handle my business anymore, would you handle it?' And I said, 'Sure, I'd be glad to.'

"And it wasn't long before he became involved in a corporate transaction that I knew damn well I had no business handling. So I referred it to a corporate lawyer who could handle it. And Bill just raised hell with me. He said, 'I believe in having one lawyer. I don't want anybody else fooling with my business.' And I said, 'I'm not going to do it. If you don't want somebody who knows what they're doing, then you can go someplace else.'

"So he begrudgingly agreed to let me refer it to my corporate partner as long as I would sit there with him, which was a total waste of my time and his money because I didn't have the foggiest idea how to answer the questions that had to be answered in order to properly handle that transaction. That worked out very well and he was really pleased. And within about a year I had several lawyers working for him.

"After a round of golf one day, as we were having a scotch, he told me that it was the first time in his life he had really efficient representation. And I said, 'Well, I'm glad that you finally confessed that I knew what I was talking about when I said that one lawyer shouldn't handle all your business.'"

Mr. Love took the concept of specialization even further. When he took over as the manager of the litigation department, he organized the department by specialty sections. Many people objected strongly to the further division of litigation into specialties.

"Clients who are hiring want lawyers who already know what they are doing and are successful at it. And to know what you're doing and have that reputation, you must to some degree at least specialize so that you are known to be one of the best in that one particular area of law.

Specialization worked well at Powell Goldstein's trial department. "Law is too complex to try to be a specialist in every area that we're called upon to litigate. There are certain general-type cases that anybody who knows how to litigate can handle. All you need to know is how to get to the courthouse and file interrogatories and answer interrogatories and that sort of thing. But if you're dealing with an anti-trust case or libel and slander or intellectual property et cetera, you should know what you're doing when you start."

Mr. Love recalls a situation in which he did not know what he was doing. "Early in my practice I had a panic situation I'm never going to forget. I was hired in two anti-trust cases, and I hadn't even had the course in law school. One of them involved several big corporate defendants. And I'm talking to all these anti-trust lawyers in Texas and New York and I didn't know what the hell they were talking about.

"While this was going on, I got a notice from Emory University. They were offering

*Frank Love Jr. during his early days at Powell, Goldstein, Frazer & Murphy, circa 1955.*

a course in anti-trust. You go at night, three nights a week for two hours. I immediately signed up. I rapidly learned enough so at least I knew what my cohorts were talking about. I probably shouldn't have taken these cases at all. If I were doing it now, I would have referred them to someone in the firm who does anti-trust work. But at that time we didn't have such people to refer it to, so I became a specialist in a hurry."

What happens if your specialty is not currently in demand? The benefit of being in a career for close to sixty years is the perspective you gain on the cycles the economy goes through. Mr. Love has lived through two to three major recessions during his time of practicing law.

"If you're specializing in an area and the business just dries up, which happens sometimes, you have to learn new skills," he advised. "You have to take some cases that you wouldn't take ordinarily, both from a standpoint of money and skill requirements. When the economy is bad, litigation explodes. And when the economy is good, litigation goes down and corporate goes up. That's not 100 percent true, but that's generally what happens.

"Once we were in a serious recession and many of the corporate people didn't have anything to do. The litigation department had more than we could handle. I had a couple of bright young corporate lawyers taking depositions and arguing motions. Of course we had to give them a quick training on how to do that, but they performed nobly in that period over a year or two when they had little else to do.

"A lot of people practice law solo or with the small firms that don't have a variety of business and that's a

*A good way to get new clients is to ask existing clients for new business, Mr. Love advises.*

real problem. Practicing law in a big firm or a small firm is so different. It's just like day and night. But several things are clear and that's that specialization is the way to go now, and it always was, except few knew it."

Although much has changed in the practice of law in the past half-century, one thing remains unquestionably the same: the need to attract clients. Mr. Love always tells young lawyers that to do so, people have to know you, one way or another.

"You have to do something," he said. "You can't just sit around, read books, then go home, have a drink, and go to bed, because if people don't know you, they're not going to hire you, and if other lawyers don't know you, they are not going to refer business to you."

Going to school in Georgia and being active while you are there gives you a head start, he believes, because the lawyers in Georgia will know you. "But if you go to school at Yale, Harvard, or at Washington and Lee as I did, then there are not many lawyers in Georgia who are going to know who you are. And you better let them find out." He recommends activities with the bar associations as one way to get to know other lawyers.

But he recommends you know business people as well. "I was active in the Sandy

Springs Community Association," he said. "I didn't do that necessarily with the idea of getting business but I did it to help a zoning situation that I was very much involved in. But I never would have gotten all those condemnation cases had people not known whom I was and what I did. And if I hadn't gotten those cases, then I wouldn't have gotten all the condemnation cases that came into the firm. So if I had just gone home and played with the kids, played tennis with my wife and so forth, I wouldn't have had that business."

He has an additional piece of advice for attorneys who may have been in practice for a few years: tell your clients you are looking for more business.

"Just say to them, 'Would you please recommend me if you have a chance?' You'd be amazed that unless you tell somebody that they won't think of it. But if you do tell them that, the chances are very good that that client, if he's happy with you, which is of course the number one requirement, will send you some clients. Happy clients are a good source of business.

"I was hired in two major cases in Georgia for the American Legion because the adjutant general of the Legion was employed in the general counsel's office of Mobil Oil during the time I was working for them and remembered my name."

Mr. Love admits that building a practice now can be very tough, partly because there are so many more lawyers. "It takes a lot of effort and a lot of time to build a practice. You don't always make it home in time to see the kids."

He also recommends taking clients out now and then. "It's funny, as many cases as I tried, I always found time to play golf or go to dinner with clients. I'm not sure anybody today is working any harder than I did. I tried twenty or thirty, forty jury cases a year, for years. Of course they were not all big cases. Many were things like rear-end collisions. But some of them were big – death cases and so forth – and I never was not busy. But you can find time to take a client to lunch. You're going to eat lunch, and I never did believe in eating lunch on your desk."

Once you have the clients, other than an occasional lunch, what else should you do to maintain the relationship? Although Mr. Love counts many friends among his clients, he didn't necessarily try to establish a family-type relationship with everyone he represented. When he was discussing business with a client, he would ask about their families as a matter of conversation, and sometimes would go to dinner or play golf with a client.

> Mr. Love admits that building a practice now can be very tough, partly because there are so many more lawyers.

"I guess some lawyers spend most of their time entertaining clients. In fact I know some lawyers who do little but entertain clients. But they're in firms where management can say 'You go entertain clients and we'll handle the business.'"

Mr. Love considers his wife, Libby, one of the assets to his career. "I was fortunate enough to have a wife who loved people and loved to go to socialize and make new friends. She was never short on conversation. When we took clients to dinner I never had to say a word. I just sat down and smiled."

Libby even charmed actor Mickey Rooney and his wife, Jan. "I was representing WXIA at the time. They wanted to interview Mickey Rooney, but he said he would only do it if he could have the interview at Peachtree Golf Club. So I arranged that, and after the interview Mickey and I played golf with the clients. The next day Mickey and I played golf again and my wife, Libby, and his wife, Jan, tagged along. Before they left town Mickey sent Libby one hundred roses."

Mr. Love said you can establish a personal relationship with a client by talking to them on the telephone. "One of the big problems I have is with all this electronic communication. Instead of picking up the phone and talking to client, you send an e-mail. There are two things wrong with that. One, it creates a record of whatever you said that is difficult to get rid of. And two, it's not a personal thing. You don't get a personal response. You get another e-mail in response. And oftentimes they're misconstrued. And so I never did that.

## In addition to using the phone rather than e-mail, Mr. Love believes you always need to make sure the client is getting attention.

"If I had something to say to the client, I'd pick up the phone and talk to them. Or take them to lunch and talk to them. Of course, one reason was that I was never very good at sending e-mails. And a better reason is that during most of the years I practiced there was no such thing. But I really think that that's a problem of the profession. Being wedded to a computer is certainly a convenient thing and certainly efficient in many ways. But it does interfere with a personal relationship between lawyer and client. Too much, I think."

In addition to using the phone rather than e-mail, Mr. Love believes you always need to make sure the client is getting attention. If you have several lawyers working for one of your clients, make sure whoever you have referred them to is communicating, doing what needs to be done, and that the client understands the cost element involved.

"Sometimes that's easy and sometimes it's not. That's the way people in this firm have handled client business forever."

And how do you deal with a dissatisfied client? "The client is always right, period. There's no such thing as 100 percent certainty about anything, certainly some clients make stupid mistakes no matter what you tell them. But I think that's the exception rather than the rule. If the client knows the consequences of doing this, that, and the other and has it in writing, then of course the client is the ultimate arbiter of what's done, and there's nothing you can do about that."

Mr. Love emphasizes that it is extremely important for the client to have an accurate view of the circumstances. You're responsible to make sure the client has both sides of the story and makes a judgment based on knowledge of the consequences.

Above all, Mr. Love said, is that you never want a client to be surprised. "There is a tendency to be overly optimistic about what you can do for a client," he said. "The client has got to understand the upside and downside. Whether it's litigation or a corporate deal or whatever. And you cannot be so full of life that you give a client a slanted view of what his chances are of being successful on whatever the project is, so that if it goes sour, it's a total surprise to him. In most instances you can just kiss that client goodbye. They've got to know that there's a downside if there is. And there almost always is, although it may be slight, but you've got to communicate with your client the upside and the downside of whatever it is that's going on, whether it's litigation or possible merger or whatever. What are the chances that you're going to be successful – an honest view of that – and what are the chances that you won't, and if you're not, what's going to happen. All this with the understanding that if a clients wants to get from point A to point B your job is to get the client from point A to point B safely."

He also advises attorneys to know where to draw the line. "Sometimes you've got a demanding client – and I've had them, just like everybody else – who insists that you do something stupid. It is perfectly permissible to say to the client, 'No, I am not going to do that. If that's what you want to do, you get somebody else to do it.' And make sure you are perfectly clear both verbally and in writing that you are no longer representing that client in connection with that matter."

Although he has a few clients complain about a bill or a fee, that has been rare. In fact, he tells the story of client who thought he hadn't paid enough.

"A client once told me to tear the bill up, and to send him a bill for ten thousand dollars more. He said we hadn't billed him enough. How about that? And what do you think I did? I tore the bill up, added ten thousand dollars, and sent it back! Well, now, it's funny. We didn't win that case. We didn't lose it, but it was a complicated legal case. The client understood that our chances of succeeding on the legal issue, which meant several hundred thousand dollars, were slim. I thought it was worth a try, and he agreed. We did not win it. But I think he was impressed with the fact that he got an honest, straightforward view of what was going to happen or might happen, and that I worked my buns off trying to make it come out right."

> Above all, Mr. Love said, is that you never want a client to be surprised.

Mr. Love once received a wooden rooster from a client for another case he lost. "She sent me this pretty hand-carved rooster because she said I was like a little gamecock, I fought so hard. And I've got a little portable bar that a client sent me in a case that I lost, too."

But the most cherished gift from a client? "The ten thousand dollars," he said, without hesitation.

# Summary

- In order to attract clients, people have to know you, one way or another. "You have to do something," Mr. Love said. "You can't just sit around, read books, then go home, have a drink, and go to bed, because if people don't know you, they're not going to hire you, and if other lawyers don't know you, they are not going to refer business to you."

- Take clients out. "Take time to play golf once in a while and take clients out once in a while. You can find time to take a client to lunch. You're going to eat lunch, and I never did believe in eating lunch on your desk."

- Make sure the client is receiving attention. This is especially true if you have several lawyers working for one of your clients. Make sure that whomever you have referred them to is communicating, doing what needs to be done, and that the client understands the time element involved in what's going on.

- The client is always right, period. "If the client knows the consequences of doing this, that, and the other and has it in writing, then of course the client is the ultimate arbiter of what's done, and there's nothing you can do about that."

- If you've been in business a few years, tell your current clients you are looking for more business. Ask them to recommend you. "Clients who can refer cases are a very good source of business."

- If you are specializing in an area of law that is suffering with the economy, you have to learn new skills. "You have to take some cases that you wouldn't take ordinarily, both from a standpoint of money and skill requirements. When the economy is bad, litigation explodes. And when the economy is good, litigation goes down and corporate goes up."

- The client must have an accurate view of whatever is going on. The client should never be surprised. "If you're responsible for the client you've got to make sure that he has both sides of the story and makes a judgment based on knowledge of that."

- Know where to draw your line. "Sometimes you've got a demanding client – and I've had them, just like everybody else – who insists that you do something stupid. It is perfectly permissible to say to the client, 'No, I am not going to do that.'"

# Frank Love Jr.

*Frank Love Jr. is a retired partner with Powell Goldstein and former chairman of the firm's litigation department. He specialized in commercial litigation, including First Amendment rights, professional and product liability, personal injury, sports and entertainment, patent infringement, and condemnation proceedings. Mr. Love is experienced in mediation and arbitration and is a panelist with the American Arbitration Association and Closure ADR Group.*

*Mr. Love has conducted nearly two dozen seminars on trial skills for Georgia's Institute for Continuing Legal Education. He has written numerous articles for the Institute's publications as well as for the Georgia Defense Lawyers Journal.*

*In 2003 he received the Distinguished Service Award, the highest honor awarded by the State Bar of Georgia for "conspicuous service to the cause of jurisprudence and to the advancement of the legal profession in the state of Georgia."*

*Mr. Love served as president of the State Bar from 1982 to 1983, was elected to the American College of Trial Lawyers and is a life fellow of the American Bar Foundation. He has served as president of the Georgia Defense Lawyers Association and as chair of the Fifth Congressional District of the Republican Party of Georgia.*

*Mr. Love is a member of the Atlanta Bar Association, the American Bar Association, the Lawyers Club of Atlanta, and the Old War Horse Lawyers Club. He also served as a trustee of the Eleventh Circuit Historical Society and is a former president of that organization.*

# Carl E. Sanders

Founder and Chairman Emeritus
Troutman Sanders
Governor, State of Georgia, 1963-1967

Governor Carl Sanders was inspired to become a lawyer after he served for three years as a B-17 bomber pilot in World War II. He had discovered it was the lawyers who made decisions and got things done.

"When I was discharged I realized that the people who made the major decisions about whether we go to war, whether we don't go to war, or whether we do other things – most of them were lawyers. Having come to the conclusion that lawyers were very active in the affairs of government and the affairs of everyday lives, I decided that I would like to be a lawyer."

During his career, Governor Sanders was not only a lawyer, he was also involved in politics, business, and real estate. But no matter what area he was in, he got to the decision-makers and got things done. Whether that meant being involved in bringing every major sports franchise to Atlanta, or helping Ted Turner become a media mogul, Tom Cousins a real estate tycoon, and J.B. Fuqua the head of a broadcasting conglomerate, Governor Sanders was there representing all of them, as well as many other clients, both large and small.

He became the decision-maker himself for the state of Georgia, having entered politics for practical reasons. Frustrated by the party in power in Augusta that was seen as wasteful and inefficient, he ran for State House of Representatives, which led to him becoming the governor of Georgia at the age of just thirty-seven.

Governor Sanders still practices law with Troutman Sanders, as the firm that he founded in 1967 is now known. His long and successful career started with building a reputation as a good lawyer and always following his gubernatorial campaign slogan: Honesty, Integrity, Dependability.

After graduating from law school at the University of Georgia, Governor Sanders returned to his hometown of Augusta, where he began practicing law with Fred Kennedy and Henry Hammond in the firm Hammond, Kennedy and Sanders. He was primarily a trial lawyer, trying mostly plaintiffs' cases.

"I acquired the reputation that if somebody had a problem, and it needed to go to trial, then I was the lawyer to take the case to trial, and not try to settle it before it went to court. So many lawyers back then would take a case and represent to the client that they would take it to court and try it if they had to, but they really didn't want to do that, and they'd wind up settling before they ever even got to the courtroom. But I didn't do that. So as a result, I built up a good reputation and had clients coming to me and also had people referring clients to me. I successfully built a law practice by trying a lot of cases.

"It was an interesting experience. I didn't make a lot of money at that time, but I had an interesting career in front of juries and judges, and I enjoyed it. I wasn't a specialist because I couldn't afford to be. I had to be prepared to take whatever cases I thought I could do some good with and bone up on the facts, bone up on the law, get ready to go to court and try the case."

Governor Sanders said that the situation is different now for trial lawyers, but back then they didn't need to try to find clients. "In those days, if you got a reputation of being a good trial lawyer, you had plenty of cases. The cases would come to you and you could pick and choose."

But these days, he advises that anyone who wants to be a good lawyer needs to decide what type of lawyer he or she wants to be. "There's no room for generalists anymore. If you want to be a good lawyer, you have to specialize in some area of the law that you are familiar with and that you can become very good at. Therefore I think lawyers have got to decide what kind of law they're going to practice."

In a large firm like Troutman Sanders, it is easier for a lawyer to discover a specialty, particularly if he or she participates in the summer internship program. "We recruit law clerks while they are still in law school, as summer interns. We invite them to help the other lawyers during the summer to learn about the areas of law that they think they are interested in. And we try to expose them to areas they think they want to practice law in. If they find out for themselves that it's not really what they thought it was, we try to accommodate them by putting them in another section that they might be interested in. That's the best way for a young lawyer to determine whether he wants to be a corporate lawyer, an environmentalist, a trial lawyer, a real estate lawyer or a trust and estates lawyer. He can touch all those areas and really determine what his final choice might be when he settles down at a big firm or a small firm and proceeds to practice law."

> In a large firm like Troutman Sanders, it is easier for a lawyer to discover a specialty, particularly if he or she participates in the summer internship program.

After determining to focus on a particular area of law, a lawyer has another question to ask: how hard is he or she willing to work to be really successful? "I've seen too many good lawyers never become great lawyers because they were never willing to work hard enough to become a great lawyer," he said. "Good lawyers can be run-of-the-mill. They can handle most things, but when they get a real tough issue or tough case, there are not too many good lawyers that are willing to take those cases and stick with them and do whatever they have to do to conclude those cases successfully. There are just too many people who want to take the easy road and do what they can to make a living, but avoid the tough, rough, hard cases, that you face either in the boardroom or the courtroom."

Governor Sanders also believes you have to be loyal to your clients, no matter what. Sometimes economic times are tough, and you have to be willing to work with your clients when their businesses have difficulties.

"You've got to understand that clients have their ups and downs," he said. "And when they have those problems, if you are the kind of lawyer that you ought to be, you work with them. You pull back on expenses, you pull back on fees. You work with the client as they pull through this economic cycle. And unless you're able to do that, you're not going to develop the kind of clients that you like to have.

"I remember in Atlanta, in the early seventies and eighties, when the real estate market went to pieces, we worked with some clients who are wonderful clients today. But back then, they were virtually out of business. And we said to them, look, we understand your problem, we'll work with you, we'll stay with you until things get better, and we'll continue to work on this project that you are involved with.

*Governor Sanders and his wife, Betty. They met at the University of Georgia and were married in 1947. They have two children, Betty Sanders Botts and Carl Sanders Jr., six grandchildren, and one great-grandchild.*

"If you can't be loyal to your clients, you shouldn't take them on as a client. My clients have stuck with me as well and I've had some wonderful experiences and some wonderful relationships. I don't have any clients that left me and my law firm because they felt like I was not treating them fair and right."

A good lawyer can understand the client's problem better than the client does and has to be able to evaluate the problem and advise the client. "You've got to be honest and explain to him or her what the problems are and what the parameters are and how we are going to attack the situation to resolve it."

Governor Sanders also believes that if you can't be responsive and available to your client, then you shouldn't take the matter to start with. "Clients can get difficult themselves, and a lawyer has got to understand that every client may not be an easy individual to deal with but once you accept the matter and you accept it in good faith, you've got to stick with it."

He has had to walk away from clients when they wouldn't accept his advice. "I explained to the client what I thought was needed to handle the problem, and if he or he or she then said, 'We can't accept that, we want you to do it this way, not the way you've described it,' then I'd say, 'I can't do it your way. I have to do it my way, and therefore the best thing for us to do is to part company.'"

That is just one example of Governor Sanders' integrity, which he believes is crucial to a lawyer. "If you don't have integrity, if you can't look a judge in the face or any other lawyer in the face and tell him or her how you feel and what you are trying to do, and do it with honesty and integrity, then you shouldn't be practicing law."

In fact it was his sense of integrity and honesty that led him into politics, which led to his becoming the youngest governor in the country at that time. Although he had harbored no political ambitions previously, he went into politics for a practical reason: to get things done.

*Carl Sanders was just thirty-seven when he was elected governor of Georgia, the youngest governor in the country. He was considered a voice of calm and reason in a time of upheaval.*

"Augusta had been run politically by a group that called themselves the Cracker Party, and they were sort of similar to Tammany Hall in New York. They controlled anybody who wanted a job in the city or the county. You had to go through the Cracker Party in order to get something done. When I became the first pilot of a B-17 bomber with a ten-man crew, I realized that sometimes you had to take a stand and do something different than what you might think otherwise. So some of us veterans decided that we were not going to live in Augusta under the Cracker Party. We formed the Independent Party and put candidates against the old Crackers and beat them. That's why I got into politics. The county and the city were locked up in a political situation that was not good for anybody. So we beat them and I went to the House and Senate, and later to the governorship."

Governor Sanders was elected to the Georgia House of Representatives in 1954, representing the people of Richmond County. He served one term in the House, then three terms in the Senate. In 1962, he ran for governor and served from 1963 to 1967. During his term he improved the infrastructure, helped reform several government agencies such as the Highway Department, Department of Agriculture, the prison system, and the state merit system, and courted foreign industry.

Education was a top priority and in addition to working on the public schools, he opened new junior colleges and a dental school and appropriated more money for the university system. More than two billion dollars was invested in education during his term.

During a time of racial unrest, Governor Sanders led the transition toward racial desegregation, cooperating with John F. Kennedy and Lyndon B. Johnson on complying with civil rights laws. He was also instrumental in building several airports around the state. During his term he became friends with both President Kennedy and President Johnson.

Unable to succeed himself as governor, Governor Sanders left office. Although President Johnson offered him several national positions, he declined.

As a man who likes to get things done, he didn't think he could accomplish what he would like at the national level. "I never wanted to go to Washington and serve," he said. "When I was governor, I appointed a speaker. I appointed committees. I ran the state. We accomplished more than anybody ever thought about accomplishing. And I ran it like a business. People urged me to go to Washington, but I said no. I know how it operates in Washington. You go up there and you sit. If you go to the Senate, you sit for twelve years or longer before you get enough influence to do anything. You vegetate. I didn't want to do that. A couple of former governors who served in Washington told me, 'Boy, this is the worst job we ever had. I wish we were back in the governor's office.' So that's why I never had any aspirations to go and serve in Washington; it just wasn't my cup of tea."

With his reputation and his accomplishments as governor, Governor Sanders could have walked right out of the Governor's Mansion into a plush office as a partner in any law firm in Atlanta. Instead, he chose to start his own firm, and with three lawyers founded Sanders Ashmore & Boozer, with offices in the Commerce Building. In 1972 the firm merged with Troutman, Sams, Schroder and Lockerman to form Troutman Sanders. When its merger with Washington DC-based Ross, Dixon & Bell is complete in January 2009, the firm will have 750 attorneys located in fifteen cities on three continents. "We've grown nicely," Governor Sanders said.

As a former governor, it wasn't hard for him to attract clients to his new firm. "The fact that I'd had a very successful administration as governor, that I had run the state like the CEO of a big company, and I had gotten programs passed that I had promised to get passed and gotten educational reform, was impressive to companies in private life."

> ## "We accomplished more than anybody ever thought about accomplishing."

Clients figured if the governor could run the state and also leave a surplus of one hundred forty million dollars in the state coffers, they would be in good hands. But he did have to give up trying cases. "When I was practicing law before, a long case might be two or three weeks. When I came out of the governor's office and started my law firm, a long case might be two or three years. So instead of being able to go to the courtroom as I had done previously, I had to switch and become counsel, advisor, and director. I had to change from the courtroom to the boardroom."

One of the firm's early clients was First Georgia Bank. Delta Air Lines and the Food Giant grocery chain were also big clients. Although his firm handled plenty of well-known clients, not all of them were rich or successful, at least in the beginning. Media mogul Ted Turner was an early client, and remains one to this day.

One of Governor Sanders' oldest friends was the late J.B. Fuqua, who ran his campaign for governor in 1962 and became a life-long client as he built up his broadcasting empire of Fuqua Companies.

Troutman Sanders also represented Tom Cousins, at that time a young real estate developer who founded Cousins Properties with his father in 1958. He went on to become a real estate tycoon and one of the most influential business leaders in the history of Atlanta.

Governor Sanders believes that to be successful, you have to do more than just handle matters that someone brings to you, and you have to work hard to help your clients achieve their goals. "Secondly, to be really successful, you have to take some risks," he said. "You can't expect people to come knock on your door, with you not having taken any risks. You have to be willing to go with a Ted Turner, go with a Tom Cousins, go with a Southern Company or the Georgia Power Company, even though at times you might think, well, I'm not going to get much out of this, and that's the risky thing. And it doesn't always work out, but if you're not willing to take some risks, you're not likely to get the reward you'd like to get."

Governor Sanders also did a great deal of work for Georgia Power Company, an account that came with the 1972 merger with Troutman, Sams, Schroder and Lockerman. But he was able to get a bigger part of that business by going after it.

"The Southern Company, which owned the Georgia Power Company, used a New York law firm for all of their bond business. So I went to see [the late] Alvin Ward Vogtle, who was the president of the Southern Company. He was a good man and tough as nails. He had been shot down in World War II and served two years in a prison camp. He was the inspiration for the lead POW character in the movie *The Great Escape*. I said, 'Alvin, we can do your bond business cheaper than a New York law firm, and we can do it here, in Atlanta, where your headquarters are.' He thought about it and he finally called me and gave me permission.

"So I had the delicate duty of going to New York, sitting down with the executive committee of one of the big law firms, and saying, 'Our client wants us to continue to work together, but we will become lead counsel and you will be local counsel on the bond work.'"

Because of his friendship with President Lyndon Johnson, Governor Sanders was also able to help Delta Air Lines obtain regulatory approval to fly directly to Honolulu. That was when the Civil Aeronautics Bureau was still in existence.

# While Governor Sanders was in office, Mayor Ivan Allen started a campaign to bring a Major League Baseball team to Atlanta.

In addition to all of his accomplishments as governor and as a lawyer, Governor Sanders is also known for another achievement that has changed the city forever – bringing major league sports to Atlanta.

While Governor Sanders was in office, Mayor Ivan Allen started a campaign to bring a Major League Baseball team to Atlanta. In an effort to attract the Braves from Milwaukee, Allen wanted to construct a stadium. The city had acquired the property, but there was no highway access to it. Through his efforts with the Highway Department, Governor Sanders was able to get the necessary overpass road to the stadium built. The stadium was constructed in less than a year and the Braves came to Atlanta in 1966.

Also while Mr. Sanders was governor, Pete Rozelle, National Football League commissioner, told him that he wanted a franchise in Atlanta and asked if he knew of anyone who would purchase a team. Governor Sanders recommended his fraternity brother, Rankin Smith, who loved football and more important, had the money. Even when the price rose to a record eight-and-a-half million dollars, Governor Sanders still urged his friend to buy the franchise, which he did in 1965 and named the team the Atlanta Falcons. It was good advice; Mr. Rankin's family sold the franchise in 2001 to Arthur Blank for $545 million.

*Governor Sanders' office at Troutman Sanders contains mementos from his long career. Serving as a B-17 bomber pilot in World War II led to his decision to become a lawyer. A portion of I-20 near the South Carolina border is named after Governor Sanders, who was born in Augusta.*

The next professional team to come was the Atlanta Hawks. Tom Cousins approached Governor Sanders with his idea to build a coliseum downtown for basketball and other events. "He asked me, 'Do you think there's any way I can do that?' I said, 'I'll see what I can find out.'"

The owner of the St. Louis Hawks was willing to sell, but building a stadium would take two to three years. So Governor Sanders worked out a deal with Coach Bobby Dodd at Georgia Tech and the Board of Regents for the Hawks to play at Tech until the Omni was built. Governor Sanders and Tom Cousins brought the Hawks to Atlanta in 1968, the first National Basketball Association team in the Deep South. The Omni was completed in 1972. That year, Tom Cousins brought ice hockey to town with the purchase of the Flames from the National Hockey League. He offered a part ownership to Governor Sanders (who owned 10 percent of the Hawks to Tom Cousin's 90 percent), but he declined, saying he had enough ownership, but he'd be glad to represent him. Cousins sold the Hawks to Ted Turner in 1977 and then sold the Atlanta Flames to a Canadian investor in 1980.

Governor Sanders also represented Tom Cousins in recommending that the state government create an authority to build the World Congress Center. Governor Sanders says that it was a tough sell in the early seventies, but it has been a tremendous economic generator for downtown Atlanta.

At the age of eighty-three, Governor Sanders is still active in his law firm, although he finally gave up some of the management duties when he chose Bob Webb as managing partner in 1994. "I'm proud of our firm and I'm proud of him. The only thing I don't like is that when I get on the elevator, I don't know whether I'm looking at a client or a partner, associate, or some guy who got on the elevator by mistake. You can't have that intimate personal relationship with more than 700 lawyers."

Governor Sanders believes Troutman Sanders has plenty of all three types of lawyers: finders, minders, and grinders. "The best lawyer you can have is one that can find the business," he said. "The next is the one who can mind the business when it's found. Then you can find some good lawyers who can neither find or mind it, but grind it out. And we got plenty of all of them."

But how do you get to be a finder? According to Governor Sanders, "You get elected governor, and you demonstrate that you can run the state."

Obviously, that isn't possible for most people, but he says if you aren't in the political arena you can still demonstrate your skill. "You have to demonstrate that you're capable of good advice and hard work for somebody to want to give you something to work on, and that's the only way I know how to do it. If they don't know who you are and you haven't demonstrated it by going to court and trying cases and you haven't demonstrated it by going to the boardroom and developing a plan to acquire other companies, you're not going to have the kind of clientele that will provide you with a good living and build a good law firm.

## Governor Sanders said that setbacks often can lead to even better opportunities.

"You've got to give them good service, you make them realize how important they are to you and you work as hard as you can work in every way that you can to accomplish their goals. As long as you provide your clients with the kind of service that they need and demonstrate to them that you're willing to pay the price no matter what it takes in terms of time and effort, they'll stay with you. You will get to the point where you will be such an intimate advisor, they're not gonna leave you."

And his clients didn't. One of the firm's now retired partners, Tench Coxe, represented Ted Turner from the time he first inherited his father's outdoor billboard company and the firm was with him along the way as he built his media empire. When Mr. Turner wanted CNN to join the White House press corps so he'd have access for the fledgling news network, the major networks didn't want him or his network there. So in 1981, Troutman Sanders filed an antitrust lawsuit against the three main broadcast TV networks that ultimately granted CNN access to the White House news pool, paving the way for the CNN of today.

"We demonstrated that we had the capability of doing what he wanted to do, and we had the intestinal fortitude to file suits against the White House press corps and everyone associated with it. If you demonstrate to a client that you'll go through hell or high water for him to achieve a legitimate purpose, he'll be your client from then on."

Governor Sanders said setbacks often can lead to even better opportunities. "The road to success is not going to always be smooth as silk and you are going to have bumps. You've got to be willing to take those bumps and keep plugging away. Be honest, be fair, work hard, and don't quit, no matter how tough things get."

# Summary

- Establish a good reputation. "I acquired the reputation that if somebody had a problem, and it needed to go to trial, then I was the lawyer to take the case to trial, and not try to settle it before it went to court."

- Decide what kind of lawyer you'll be. "There's no room for generalists anymore. If you want to be a good lawyer, you have to specialize in some area of the law that you are familiar with and that you can become very good at."

- Decide how hard you are willing to work to be successful. "I've seen too many good lawyers never become great lawyers because they were never willing to work hard enough to become a great lawyer. Good lawyers can be run-of-the-mill. They can handle most things, but when they get a real tough issue or tough case, there are not too many good lawyers who are willing to take those cases and stick with them and do whatever they have to do to conclude those cases successfully."

- Be loyal to your clients, no matter what. When they are going through tough economic times, work with them. "You've got to understand that clients have their ups and downs. And when they have those problems, if you are the kind of lawyer that you ought to be, you work with them. You pull back on expenses, you pull back on fees. You work with the client as they pull through this economic cycle."

- Demonstrate your skill as a lawyer. "You have to demonstrate that you're capable of good advice and hard work for somebody to want to give you something to work on, and that's the only way I know how to do it."

- Work as hard as you can work in every way that you can to accomplish your clients' goals. "As long as you provide your clients with the kind of service that they need and demonstrate to them that you're willing to pay the price no matter what it takes in terms of time and effort, they'll stay with you. You will get to the point where you will be such an intimate advisor, they're not going to leave you."

- To be successful you have to work harder than other people and be willing to take risks, including helping clients in the early days of their careers. "You have to be willing to go with a Ted Turner, go with a Tom Cousins, go with a Southern Company or the Georgia Power Company, even though at times you might think, well, I'm not going to get much out of this, and that's the risky thing. And it doesn't always work out, but if you're not willing to take some risks, you're not likely to get the reward that you'd like to get."

- Be honest, be fair, work hard, and don't quit, no matter how tough things get.

# Carl E. Sanders

Carl E. Sanders is Chairman Emeritus of Troutman Sanders, one of the largest and most prestigious law firms in Atlanta, Georgia. The firm is composed of approximately 700 attorneys.

Governor Sanders also remains active in public life, leading civic and philanthropic causes. He is a past chairman of the Japan-America Society of Georgia. In 1996, when Atlanta hosted the Olympics, he served as a member of the Atlanta Committee for the Olympic Games, and was an Olympic Torch Bearer in Augusta. He is a World War II Veteran who served as a B-17 bomber pilot.

He was governor of Georgia from 1963 to 1967 during a time of spectacular social and economic change. He received national attention as "one of the new breed of Southern politicians" who was a "voice of calm and reason in a sea of upheaval." He was a member of the Executive Committee of the National Governors Conference, and chairman of the Southern Regional Education Board. He was chairman of the Southern Governors Conference in 1965. Prior to becoming Governor, he served one term in the Georgia House of Representatives and three terms in the Georgia State Senate. He was President Pro Tem of the State Senate from 1960 to 1963.

In November 1989, the emperor and government of Japan bestowed upon Governor Sanders the very prestigious Order of the Sacred Treasure, Gold and Silver Award, for significant contributions to promote friendly relations between the United States and Japan.

Governor Sanders was also a fellow at John F. Kennedy School of Government at Harvard University; member of the U. S. Intergovernmental Relations Commission of Federal/State Relations from 1963 to 1965; chairman of the Rules Committee of the Democratic National Convention in 1964; appointed by President Lyndon B. Johnson to the National Commission on Urban Affairs, Advisory Council Office of Economic Opportunity in 1967; member of the National Citizens Committee for Public Television in 1969; appointed by the president and confirmed by the United States Senate as a member of the board of directors of the Public Broadcasting Corporation from 1968 to 1970; and served on the Commission on the Operation of the United States Senate in 1976.

Governor Sanders is a native of Augusta, Georgia, and a graduate of the University of Georgia, where he received the Juris Doctor Degree. He and his wife, the former Betty Bird Foy of Statesboro, Georgia, reside in Atlanta. They have two children, six grandchildren, and one great-grandchild.

# Richard Sinkfield

Founding Partner
Rogers & Hardin

$M$ost people think of a client as the person or company that hires them to provide a service. But when Richard Sinkfield discusses his philosophy of client service, he expands the traditional meaning of who is a client. He believes that in a law firm, the partner you work for and in many instances, the lawyer on the other side should also be treated as clients.

Although he didn't realize it at the time, Mr. Sinkfield developed his philosophy of client service as a young associate. He realized he needed to treat a partner for whom he was working as a client.

"I realized that in order to be successful, I had to try make the partner I was working for successful. And while that sounds a little calculated, it wasn't quite like that. I discovered that if I could do a good job for the partner that I was working for, the partner would give me more work and sometimes I would get exposure directly with the client. Then maybe that client would ask for me the next time."

Initially he looked at this approach as simply survival: He had to do good work for the lawyer who assigned the task in order to keep his job.

"Then in a short period of time, I began to realize the relationship between doing the first thing well and getting the next assignment. And when I began to pick that up, I became more structured. I tell young lawyers in our offices that your first client may be me or another partner here, and you are expected to be perfect. But the reward is that when you do that, I'll be back to you. It's an honor to be overworked in the sense that people want you to do something for them. Whether it is the lawyer you are working for or the client you serve, if they come back, that is a high distinction."

Mr. Sinkfield also believes his client is in many cases the lawyer on the other side. "I don't mean to say that I'm being solicitous at the time that I am representing on the other side, but if I treat the opposing lawyers with respect and professionalism, when they have a matter for a client that has a conflict for them and they want someone to represent that client, they will think of me and our firm. That has been a lifeline for us. We are basically a referral-based firm and a great many cases that we get are referred by other lawyers."

Growing up in Montgomery, Alabama, Mr. Sinkfield didn't always dream of being a lawyer. He had participated in debate at Tennessee State A&I University, and through his fraternity, Alpha Kappa Alpha, became active in politics. It was at the suggestion of a political science teacher that he attended law school and graduated from Vanderbilt University School of Law in 1971.

*Richard Sinkfield was admitted to the International Academy of Trial Lawyers.*

He began his practice at Powell, Goldstein, Frazer & Murphy in Atlanta, where he started with a combined anti-trust and construction-bond practice. C.B. Rogers, a partner who often worked with young associates, pulled him into a securities fraud case.

Mr. Sinkfield points to that case as the most influential over his career. "I was a year out of law school at the time that the case went to trial. It was a jury trial and I was the number two person on the team. Within two years of being out of law school, C.B. let me argue the case for the then Fifth Circuit, what is now the Eleventh Circuit. He had won in the jury trial and said to me, 'Now it's your time.'

But more importantly to my career, in the course of the trial and the appeal, I learned as much about securities fraud as any lawyer in Atlanta, probably more than most. So for the next ten to fifteen years of my career, I was viewed as a 10b5 securities lawyer, which was a segue into business practice, the broader practice that I have now. Today, I have only one securities case of the commercial cases that I am handling."

In April 1976, eight lawyers at Powell Goldstein left and formed Rogers & Hardin, and Mr. Sinkfield was one of the original partners. Within eight months the firm had clients such as the City of Atlanta and major airlines.

Mr. Sinkfield found it of great help to have an older partner take an interest in his career and looks back at that experience today when he deals with the young lawyers in his firm.

"I was enormously blessed to have an opportunity to work with C.B. Rogers over the years, who always pushed me beyond what I thought I was ready to do. I have tried to do the same thing with young lawyers who I work with and to give them experiences right at the edge, and sometimes just over the edge of what they think they are ready to do. I believe that helps with growth."

A big part of working with young attorneys is teaching them to deal with clients, which includes being responsive to clients and keeping them up to date. "As a lawyer, I don't want to be surprised and clients don't want to be surprised. So number one, I try to keep clients current on what is happening in the case on a regular basis. If it is a case where we are interacting on a weekly or monthly basis, just because of the nature of the case, I don't have to do anything special. And if it is a case where we are not having interaction, maybe it is being overseen by a claims adjuster or an insurance company, then we report frequently."

Although he wonders sometimes if there is a better way to communicate than through e-mail, he does appreciate the ability to transmit information to a client instantly. "There are a lot of weeds in the lawn of e-mail. You get a lot of unsolicited stuff from different organizations, and not all spam, but you have to go through it in order to get at it. That is an added piece to communicating today. But it keeps me instantly in touch, which is the other aspect of it. I can be out of the office and my back pocket vibrates and I can look and see if it is something that I need to respond to."

For Rogers & Hardin, counseling CEOs, especially on how to be a witness, is an important part of the practice. "CEOs are typically like trial lawyers or people who are accustomed to directing and determining direction or focus and giving orders, not taking orders. When they find themselves involved in litigation, particularly when they are called upon as witnesses, it is not a very happy occasion. We also have to counsel them to look beyond the notion that this is just their opportunity for vengeance on the world. It is a great thing to have high principles, but helping them maintain a business perspective in the context of litigation is important."

Mr. Sinkfield learned in law school that lawyers also have to have honesty from their clients. "I worked with a criminal defense lawyer in Nashville, Tennessee when I was in law school. He defended a lot of youngsters on car

> **Mr. Sinkfield believes that although like the general population, clients come in all sizes, flavors and attitudes, they all want the same thing: good representation.**

theft charges. Generally he would hear the same story. The kid was walking down the street and some fellow with a nickname that he had not seen before asked him if he wanted to take it for a ride and his luck was such that during his spin around the block, cops pulled him over. He didn't steal it and didn't know it was stolen. And the lawyer would tell them, 'Son, you are not smart enough to lie. Leave the stories to the lawyer. You tell me the truth and we will figure out how to present the case.' And I think that is the truth – most clients are not smart enough to lie."

Mr. Sinkfield believes that like the general population, clients come in all sizes, flavors, and attitudes, but they all want the same thing: good representation. And to receive his best representation, they have to tell him the truth. "They really are looking for direction and leadership. They come to realize what our values are and what our purpose is, that we have their interest uppermost in mind and they can hurt themselves sometimes by tactics that are off center. There is no bad fact; there is nothing in the history of their transaction that we cannot handle in the course of the case, even if it means settling. What we cannot handle is the surprise of not knowing and the lack of candor. I tell my clients that the worst thing they can do to themselves is lie. In our world, lies get discovered."

Looking back on his career, Mr. Sinkfield feels that although a lot of things about client service have not changed, the technical tools are considerably greater and the environment is different in terms of the extent to which you establish a relationship with the decision maker. He also has seen clients seek more control and direction over what the firm charges and how many lawyers might work on a file. And he has noticed lawyers are in some instances more combative than when he started thirty years ago.

"As lawyers, particularly as litigators, we're all combative. We are all competitive, and we try to win, which means advancing the solution that really works for the client, whether it is through a jury trial or through an advantageous settlement. Now it is more personally combative. It was rare for me to get into a verbal altercation with a lawyer thirty years ago. We might have a difference of opinion, but I can't remember a situation where I thought the lawyer on the other side was actually exhibiting real temperament. Sometimes you would raise your voice for effect, but you were not angry, you were not ready to go to blows. In more recent years, and with some younger lawyers, their egos get in the way of good judgment and good behavior. I've seen them exhibit temperament from time to time, but it is not my style, and I don't tolerate it. If the lawyer wants to be abusive, he or she can do it without me. I just simply conclude that session, and when they want to deal differently, we can start over again. And it works pretty well."

## The qualities Mr. Sinkfield looks for in young lawyers are maturity, diligence, and thoroughness.

If he sees a lawyer, particularly in his firm, who he believes is a little more personally involved in an issue than good professionalism would allow, he pulls him to the side and counsels him. "I have been accused by my adversaries of counseling them also from time to time, so it kind of works both ways."

The qualities Mr. Sinkfield looks for in young lawyers are maturity, diligence, and thoroughness. He also looks for someone who is prepared to sacrifice self if necessary. "There are times in litigation when you can't always set your own schedule. And having raised two children, I know the demands of family, and we try to respect that, but there are times where we will go sixteen, eighteen, twenty hours a day during a trial. So I look for a person who recognizes the need to be involved and who is willing and prepared."

He also looks for the extent to which young lawyers vet their ideas. Mr. Sinkfield still runs his ideas by other lawyers in the office, from the youngest to the oldest if he believes they may have information that is relevant to a particular problem.

"There is great value in vetting an idea, and it is rare that I vet an idea that I don't take away something new or different from the lawyer with whom I vetted. That is a value that we provide to clients, which is why I have spent times debating with clients when they say we have too many lawyers working on the file. I tell them that we are a firm, and the way to get the value of this unit we have is to have a vehicle in which we brainstorm. I would love to believe that I had all the ideas that contributed to my success, but I know that is far from the truth. If there is anything that contributed to it, it has been the collegiality and the willingness to vet ideas. We come up with some pretty good solutions, but they are not all Sinkfield solutions."

Mr. Sinkfield looks for young lawyers with good judgment and wants them to learn how to interact with clients in a way that supports the partners.

"We rely a lot on judgment, so we try to help young lawyers by involving them in client consultations so they see our exercise of judgment or restraint or when to give advice and when not to. I like to tell young lawyers that when we are doing a joint consultation for the client, if they have some great advice that the client should hear from them, I like to hear it first. I don't like the surprise of learning something, even if it is right, the first time while we are with the client. I am looking to them for ideas and want them to treat the case as if it is their own. Bring me a solution as if it was your decision. We will then refine it and present it to the client."

In working with young African-American attorneys, he offers them one additional piece of advice, which he learned when he was a young attorney.

*During his long career, Richard Sinkfield has been active with the bar and a member of several bar committees.*

"I tell them, 'When you feel that you are being abused or mistreated or overworked, let race be the last reason you attribute that to happening. When I was two years out of law school, I was asked to argue a case for the Supreme Court of Georgia. I was a debater with the Jessup International Law Moot Court Competition in law school and had done reasonably well in that. I knew I could probably make an appellate argument and my firm knew that and they sent me over. The lawyer on the other side, who was much my senior, asked where the other two lawyers were. And I said that they were out of the office and asked me to handle it. He said, 'They must not have thought much of this case to send you over.' This was around 1973, and it crossed my mind that that was a comment based on my race, but something held me back and I didn't react. So I just said, 'What do you mean?' And he said, 'How long have you been out of law school?' I said, 'About two years.' And he said, 'Aren't you awfully young to be arguing a case in front of the Supreme Court? And I said yes and finished the argument.

"He thought it went well, from my side, not from his side, and told me. And after that, I got to know this particular lawyer. But it was just luck that I didn't challenge him on the issue of race at that point, because it did occur to me. And had I done so, I would have missed his real reason. He was saying that I was just a kid out of law school, and he was right."

Mr. Sinkfield said that in his practice in Georgia, the only time he has had anybody attack him on any basis other than the merits is when he goes to the southern part of the state. "Down there, the attorneys stand up and say in front of the jury, 'Hey, this is Mr. Sinkfield, he's that lawyer from Atlanta.' So being a lawyer from Atlanta is a bad mark if you are outside of Atlanta."

Although Mr. Sinkfield has met some clients through professional presentations, most of his clients have come through referrals from other clients. "I haven't met any clients on the golf course. Actually, in my whole life, I have never taken a full swing with a golf stick."

Once he meets a client, he tries to be a pleasant and responsible person.

"It is not uncommon to have business dinners from time to time, but I am probably not the world's most social animal. I don't regularly call up clients and take them out to dinner or to the theater or those kinds of things. But I try to maintain a pleasant disposition in the context of serving clients."

*Richard Sinkfield is a sought-after speaker at many events.*

During his career, Mr. Sinkfield has found it useful to be active with the bar and several bar committees, although he is not as active now due to time constraints.

"You get an opportunity to interact with other lawyers and that setting provides great information to me and to the other lawyer. I'll need a lawyer for example, down in south Georgia. I don't know anyone there but I was at the Board of Governors meeting and there were a few lawyers from that area that are on the Board of Governors. I have had a chance to watch them in different situations from time to time in Savannah, so they will be the first people to come to my mind. And likewise, I have had lawyers call me where their contact with me came out of that sort of situation."

He also sees participating in bar activities as an opportunity to be of service and to learn. "I've probably learned more law in the context of participating in seminars and teaching adjunct at several of the law schools than I have just in the ordinary management of the case. As a matter of fact, I would think that in my career, some of the more important principles of law that I have been able to use in nuance situations, I have discovered either in connection with seminar research or just regular update reading."

One place he has not gained clients is through his wife, Georganna Sinkfield, a member of the Georgia House of Representatives since 1982.

"Early in my career I had someone call me, and it was apparent within two minutes that they thought I might exercise some influence. It could have been offensive, but I just said, 'You are calling the wrong guy, I am probably the least influential with her, as far as legislation is concerned.' Her career as a legislator and my career as a lawyer have not crossed paths to any great degree."

Although he has been bestowed with honor upon honor for years, Mr. Sinkfield still considers it a privilege to be considered a good lawyer and for someone to hire him. "Ham Lokey used to say that the highest compliment that someone could pay you is for them to ask you to do what they cannot do for themselves. And lawyers get to do that every day and we don't always think of the privilege that we have. If you come and hire me and you want me to stand up and tell 12 people why your cause should triumph, that is a very high calling and that is an honor that we take very seriously."

# Summary

- As a young lawyer in a law firm, the first client you work for is the partner who assigns you the work. "I realized that in order to be successful, I had to try and make the partner I was working for successful. I discovered that if I could do a good job for the partner that I was working for, the partner would give me more work and sometimes I would get exposure directly with the client. Then maybe that client would ask for me the next time."

- In many instances, the lawyer on the other side should also be treated as a client. "If I treat the opposing lawyers with respect and professionalism, when they have a matter for a client that has a conflict for them and they want someone to represent that client, they will think of me and our firm."

- Keep clients up to date on how their case is progressing. "I try to keep clients current on what is happening in the case on a regular basis. If it is a case where we are interacting on a weekly or monthly basis, just because of the nature of the case, I don't have to do anything special. And if it is a case where we are not having interaction, then we report frequently."

- A lawyer must have honesty from his client. "There is no bad fact, there is nothing in the history of their transaction that we cannot handle in the course of the case, even if it means settling. What we cannot handle is the surprise of not knowing and the lack of candor."

- Young lawyers should be mature, diligent, thorough, and prepared to sacrifice to get the job done. They also should be willing to vet their ideas with other lawyers in the firm.

- Good judgment is key in a young lawyer, but it must be exercised in a way that supports the partner. "I like to tell young lawyers that when we are doing a joint consultation for the client, if they have some great advice that the client should hear from them, I like to hear it first. I don't like the surprise of learning something, even if it is right, the first time while we are with the client."

- African-American attorneys should hesitate before looking at their race as a factor if they experience a problem. "When you feel that you are being abused or mistreated or overworked, let race be the last reason you attribute that to happening."

- Bar association and other professional associations are important as a place to learn legal issues and to interact with other attorneys, who may refer business to you.

- It is a privilege to be an attorney and a high compliment to be hired by someone to do something they cannot do for themselves.

# Richard Sinkfield

*Richard H. Sinkfield, a partner with Rogers & Hardin LLP, has practiced law since 1971 with a practice emphasis in litigation and business dispute resolution, including mediation and arbitration.*

*Areas of expertise include: complex business litigation, corporate control and proxy litigation, officer/director and professional liability and governmental representation.*

*In 2003, Mr. Sinkfield and a team of Rogers & Hardin attorneys successfully represented Georgia Attorney General Thurbert Baker before the Georgia Supreme Court in a suit brought by the Governor of Georgia to compel the Attorney General to dismiss an appeal pending before the United States Supreme Court on redistricting issues. He was co-lead counsel on the defense team that successfully defended the pharmaceutical company Wyeth in a major diet drug ("phen-fen") case in Georgia.*

*Mr. Sinkfield served on the American Bar Association's Special Commission on Evaluation of Professional Standards and its standing committee on ethics and professional responsibility, participating in a six-year study and drafting process that produced the ABA Model Rules of Professional Conduct. He was special liaison to the ABA's standing committee on professional discipline and lawyers' responsibility for client protection.*

*He has been listed for more than ten years in* The Best Lawyers in America – Business Litigation. *He has been listed in Atlanta Magazine's "Top 100 Georgia Super Lawyers for 2004-2008," and as the third top vote-getter in 2004 and 2005. He has been included in the Rogers & Hardin listing in* Chambers USA, America's Leading Lawyers for Business, The Client's Guide, *for 2003 through 2008.*

*Mr. Sinkfield graduated from Tennessee A&I State University in 1968 and from Vanderbilt School of Law in 1971. He is a fellow in the American College of Trial Lawyers and the International Academy of Trial Lawyers, and is a member of the International Association of Defense Counsel. He is a member of the American Bar Association, the National Bar Association, the State Bar of Georgia, the Atlanta Bar Association, and the Gate City Bar Association.*

# Chilton Varner

Partner
King & Spalding

Chilton Varner knows a thing or two about the qualities that are important to being a good trial lawyer. A partner at King & Spalding since 1983, she has been recognized as one of the top product liability practitioners in the world and has been named as one of the top ten women litigators in the country, representing clients that include The Coca-Cola Company, the General Motors Corporation, 3M, and GlaxoSmithKline.

"One thing that no one ever mentions when they talk to you about becoming a trial lawyer is the physical stamina you need," she said. "Trying extended cases takes a tremendous physical toll and you work long hours every day. There is significant pressure, obviously, because when you have to make as many decisions as you do in the course of a trial, some of them don't work out as well as others. There is a lot of stress involved."

Another important quality is that you have to learn to move on each day. "As a trial lawyer, when things don't go so well, you've got to turn that page. You must come to court the next day and tell yourself you're going to fix anything that didn't work the day before and do a better job."

Ms. Varner said organization and preparation are keys to being a successful trial lawyer. "And an ability to just marshal all the facts and the law and to think on about six different levels at any one time. I tell people it is like playing three-dimensional chess: You've got to be thinking about what the law is, what your next question is, what the next answer is going to be, is there an objection that you need to argue to the judge in between, and what is

the jury doing? That lady on the end down here, on the second row – how is she responding to the whole interplay with this witness? So you've got to do a lot of different things well, and you have to do them very intensely from the beginning of the trial to the end."

Ms. Varner generally feels the case that means the most to her is the one she is currently handling. But she points to an automotive product liability case she handled for the defense in Kentucky as one of the most meaningful to her. After almost three weeks of trial, the jury went out for a day and a half. They came back with a verdict for the defense.

"The case involved a catastrophic injury and some difficult facts and I had not been 'first chair' all that long. It was clearly the toughest case that I had tried up to that point. It was important to me because I thought we won this difficult case because we were good teachers for the jury. Even with some challenging facts, and an enormously sympathetic case, where your heart cried out for the family that had brought the lawsuit, and even with a very able adversary on the other side, it taught me that as long as you spend time trying to be a good teacher, to explain how things work and why they work that way, you still can win."

Ms. Varner selected product liability as a focus of her practice because she saw it was a faster way to the courtroom. "I started out my first year of practice doing whatever anybody who walked through the door gave me to do. That ranged from constitutional questions to environmental law. I became involved in product liability probably in my fourth year of practice. I found that you got to the courtroom more readily with those cases, and that is what I wanted to do."

Perhaps Ms. Varner was making up for lost time. She started her career a little later than those who took a then-traditional route of going directly from undergraduate school to law school to starting practice. She spent several years between college and law school as a wife and mother.

A native of Opelika, Alabama, Ms. Varner attended Smith College in Northampton, Massachusetts. She applied only to women's colleges because she felt they were the most selective and offered the most opportunities to women. She graduated Phi Beta Kappa in 1965, and two weeks later married her college sweetheart of four years, K. Morgan Varner. They moved to Durham, North Carolina, where her husband was in his third year of law school at Duke. After his graduation, he had a ROTC commitment and they were stationed in Germany, where their daughter Ashley was born. Ms. Varner spent two years as an Army wife. The Varners moved back to the United States after the Army tour concluded, and Mr. Varner started practicing law in Atlanta.

> ## Ms. Varner generally feels that the case that means the most to her is the one she is currently handling.

When her husband left a large Atlanta firm to start his own practice, Ms. Varner helped out as his receptionist, typist and bookkeeper in the mornings when they had childcare for their daughter. "But I decided that I liked the law a lot better from his side of the desk than from my own, so I applied to law school as soon as my daughter was in school. There was no part-time law school at that time in Atlanta, so I went to Emory full-time. And I was lucky to have Emory here."

When she entered law school in the fall of 1973, Emory's law school class was more than one-third female, possibly the highest percentage of any law school in the country. "It was a diverse class, and I was by no means extraordinary."

What was out of the ordinary was going to work for King & Spalding when she graduated in 1976. She was only the second woman attorney in the then seventy-one person firm. Ms. Varner later became the first woman member of the firm's management committee and the first female litigation partner, an area she was drawn to in law school. "I liked the competi-

*Ms. Varner at the ABA Annual Meeting in Toronto with participants in the re-creation of the Sinking of the Titanic as seen through the prism of a subsequent product liability lawsuit. Ms. Varner represented the defendant, White Star Lines.*

tive part of the practice of law and I liked being on my feet. And if you like both of those things, you head for litigation."

Ms. Varner trained under three of the firm's best lawyers, who became her mentors: Judge Griffin Bell, Frank Jones, and Byron Attridge. [Please see the chapter on Griffin Bell, page seventeen.]

"Judge Griffin Bell was the former attorney general. Frank Jones had joined the law firm at age fifty as probably the best trial lawyer in Georgia at the same time that I came in as a first-year associate. Byron Attridge was chairman of the litigation section. So when I came to the firm I worked with three of the best trial lawyers in the state, in fact, in the country. The firm at that time was small enough for an associate to work directly with those partners.

"I was fortunate enough that all three of those mentors frequently asked me to work with them, so I got to watch three very different lawyers that had different strengths. I tried to figure out what it was that they did well that I could also do well, taking into account that my gender was different. It was a great opportunity for me to watch and learn how to be a good lawyer. I also learned some things about how to get business."

From her mentors and her decades of practice, Ms. Varner developed a short list of rules for business generation.

1. There are more lawyers in the marketplace than there are good clients to hire them. A savvy lawyer should always realize that she must do something better, different, more special, and more responsive, to continue to attract business. If she doesn't, the business will go to somebody who does.

2. Lawyers must be engaged in their clients' businesses. Clients want their lawyers

to understand their larger business, not just the small piece that may be involved in a particular case. And that means the lawyer must read about her clients, follow her clients' fortunes, and pay attention.

3. The first response to the client should not be "You can't do this." Clients want lawyers to tell them how they can accomplish their goals, legally and properly. You may eventually arrive at "It can't be done," but that should only be after a lot of thought and creativity. Clients want their lawyers to take their problems from them, adopt them as their own, and then solve them. That is not to say that the lawyer should make uninformed decisions; it does mean the lawyer should regard the problem as her own. Her goal is to solve it and present a satisfactory solution to the client.

4. A relationship of trust between lawyer and client allows one to be a better lawyer. Trust has to be earned, but it is well worth working for. Good relationships are far more likely to produce good results.

How does one go about becoming friends with clients? Ms. Varner believes her approach may have been different because she was a woman. Although she works with a far larger number of female clients than when she began, she still sees a predominantly male group at the upper levels of the corporations she represents.

"It doesn't work for me to try to take a client hunting, golfing, or playing tennis. The gender difference in size and strength inevitably means that that is not a terrific avenue to get business. If you are always seventy-five yards behind your client on a golf drive, you don't get to do much talking.

*Ms. Varner was the recipient of Emory Law School's Distinguished Alumni Award in 1998.*

I've always befriended clients by finding out who they are, what they are interested in, what their families are like, how old their children are, when their birthdays are. And I try to acknowledge all of those things with notes, or an exchange of books, or something that better fits the gender difference between male clients and me. With females, it is easier. It may be as simple as inviting them to the firm's retreat for women clients or it may be a special dinner or an afternoon off at the spa. There are all kinds of ways of interacting. But you need to find something that is separate from the case that you are working on." Ms. Varner also sends special notes during the holidays and at the end of the year to her clients, thanking them for their trust.

"I've been blessed over the years. I have very close friends, all over the country. And the reason that we are close friends is because I have worked with them on hard cases and challenging issues. It's been fun."

If she comes across a client who is not so easy to befriend, Ms. Varner just works harder. "It is amazing how often you can work through that. It is just a classic marketplace issue; it's not particular to lawyers. People find folks all the time that they don't get along with, and you just have to make it work. If you don't, it's not going to be as much fun and the relationship is not going to work.

Ms. Varner believes the Golden Rule of practicing law is engagement. You need to be interested in your client's business, intrigued by the challenges the case presents, and dedicated to the research and development necessary for a successful result. You need to care – deeply – about what you are doing. "There is nothing casual about what we do. Our clients entrust their fortunes and their reputations to us. That is important, and we should never forget that."

> Ms. Varner believes that in today's legal environment, marketing has become a necessary part of the practice of law.

Ms. Varner believes in today's legal environment, marketing has become a necessary part of the practice of law. She quotes a favorite statement by her mentor, Judge Griffin Bell: "It's a sorry dog that won't wag its own tail." She believes she was a beneficiary of people in her firm who introduced her to their clients, which resulted in work for her. She compares this concept to a lesson she learned from the president of Smith College during her senior year.

"They were looking for somebody to be the class fund agent for this senior class that was rolling out to enter their first year as alumni. I ended up with that job and I complained that I was not very good at going out and asking for money. The president said, 'You should remember that you should never be shy about going out and asking for money, if you believe in the institution for which you are asking.' Some of that same philosophy applies to the practice of law. If you believe that you are a good lawyer, if you believe that you and your team and your law firm can provide service that is superior, there ought to be nothing wrong or unpleasant about trying to persuade good clients of those facts."

Ms. Varner loves trying to get more good business for her law firm. "The more legal business that I can get, the better the chance I can do first-class, cutting-edge legal work. This is not just important to my reputation as a lawyer, it also means that I enjoy the lawyering more. The issues we deal with are in the news, are important to the client, and are often unresolved. The more business of that kind that I can bring into the law firm, the better off we are, the more fun we will have at what we do, and the better lawyers we will become."

Ms. Varner said King & Spalding has found two factors to be particularly effective in trying to get younger lawyers to think about business development. "The first thing is speaking and writing engagements. There are a lot of opportunities to do legal writing and legal speaking. Both can help you build your reputation. It was certainly something that I did when I was a younger lawyer. And as long as you put the effort into doing those things and doing them well, you can distinguish yourself."

The second is to involve younger lawyers in meeting with clients who have asked the firm to present to them on the firm's resources for a particular piece of business. "We have found that clients are interested in meeting the associates who will work on that matter if we are selected. It's terrific for younger lawyers to watch how the whole process works. We find that they are excited about it. They are eager to be part of the group that tries to persuade a client that we are the law firm they ought to hire."

Ms. Varner believes her gender has been an advantage in her career. "When I first started practicing, it set me apart. That's not a bad thing when you are starting out as a young lawyer. I have had perhaps a couple of incidents where I wondered if the reaction that I was drawing from a court might in some way be related to gender, but I would have to say over the long haul, I cannot think of any experience that I have had in the courtroom where I felt that I had been mistreated because of my gender. I think that's a blessing. I've talked to other women who have not been so fortunate."

Ms. Varner with daughter Ashley and Judge Griffin Bell when Ms. Varner received the Judge Learned Hand Award from the American Jewish Committee, Atlanta Chapter, on June 5, 2007.

She notes that at the beginning of her career, she was appearing in courtrooms in small towns across the South where there had never been a female practitioner before. "That meant that people's expectations were uninformed. They were cautious about what a woman practitioner would look like and act like in the courtroom. I found that as long as I did a good job, it was great, because I was remembered. If I didn't do such a great job, I was also remembered. I didn't fade into the crowd like some of my male counterparts at the firm. So that was a difference for me as a woman, but in the long run, it worked in my favor."

She felt the same benefit working with clients. "The 'contrast effect' is what psychologists call it. As long as I did a good job, I benefited from it because their expectations were either nonexistent or lower than what they got."

Ms. Varner worked hard to gain the trust of her clients and the people she encountered in the courtroom. As a product liability lawyer, she frequently worked with witnesses who had a considerable stake in the outcome of the case; for example, an automotive engineer who had designed a particular component. "If a jury found that that component had been defectively designed, the engineer's career was on the line because it was not just one product, but every car that had rolled off of the assembly line that would be found defective if things didn't go well in court. I was frequently working with engineers who had never met a woman lawyer and who didn't quite know what to make of a woman lawyer who was working in a highly technical field. They weren't sure the little lady from Atlanta would be able to understand what they did. And yet I was their lawyer. That was a great challenge. But it was also a great reward for me, when I saw them relax and begin to trust me."

She believes gender distinctions are not as great as they were when she started practice more than thirty years ago. But the main issue of balancing a career with a family remains. "That has remained peculiarly a female burden. While not exclusively a female burden, it has continued to rest more heavily on females than on males. And that just means that you need to get more out of the hours of the day. And I think women worry more, perhaps, about whether the balance is exactly the right one."

> Ms. Varner believes gender distinctions are not as great as they were when she started practice more than thirty years ago. But the main issue of balancing a career with a family remains.

Sometimes the fact she is a woman has been the basis of levity in the courtroom, including a case she had with Judge Bell. "I argued the case over in Montgomery before three judges of the Eleventh Circuit. Judge Bell knew them very well. I imagine he had a hand in the appointment of at least one of them when he was Attorney General. I was known, too, but not nearly as well as the former Attorney General. Well, Judge Bell carried my bag into the courtroom and they thought it was terrific. They ragged Judge Bell about it and they complimented me on having such a wonderful bag carrier. I still hear about it."

# Summary

- A good trial lawyer has to be organized, prepared, and able to handle the physical stamina needed for an extended trial. She also has to marshal all the facts and the law. "It is like playing three-dimensional chess ... You've got to do a lot of different things well, and you have to do them very intensely from the beginning of the trial to the end."

- A trial lawyer has to function as a teacher for the jury. "As long as you spend time trying to be a good teacher, to explain how things work and why they work that way, then you still can win a very difficult case."

- When you work with a more experienced partner, study what they do well so you can copy and transform into your own strength.

- Ms. Varner's rules of generating business for a law firm:

  1. There are more lawyers in the marketplace than there are good clients to hire them. A savvy lawyer should always realize she must do something better, different, more special, and more responsive in order to continue to attract business. If she doesn't, the business will go to somebody who does.

  2. Lawyers must be engaged in their clients' businesses. Clients want their lawyers to understand their larger business, not just the small piece that may be involved in a particular case. And that means the lawyer must read about her clients, follow her clients' fortunes and pay attention.

  3. The first response to the client should not be "You can't do this." Clients want lawyers to tell them how they can accomplish their goals, legally and properly. You may eventually arrive at "It can't be done," but that should only be after a lot of thought and creativity. Clients want their lawyers to take their problems from them, adopt them as their own and then solve them. That is not to say that the lawyer should make uninformed decisions; it does mean that the lawyer should regard that problem as her own. Her goal is to solve it and present a satisfactory solution to the client.

  4. A relationship of trust between lawyer and client allows one to be a better lawyer. Trust has to be earned, but it is well worth working for. Good relationships are far more likely to produce good results.

- Women can befriend clients through learning about them and their families. "There are all kinds of ways of interacting. But you need to find something that is separate from the case that you are working on."

• The Golden Rule of practicing law is *engagement*. You need to be interested in your client's business. "There is nothing casual about what we do. Our clients trust us with their fortunes and their reputations and that is important and we need to remember that."

• It is important to market yourself and cross-sell others in your law firm to your clients. "If you believe that you are a good lawyer, if you believe that you and your team and your law firm can provide service that is superior, there ought to be nothing wrong or unpleasant about trying to persuade good clients of those facts."

• Young lawyers should seek out writing and speaking engagements as a way to generate business. "Both of those can help you build your reputation. And as long as you put the effort into doing those things and do them well, you can distinguish yourselves."

• Partners in a firm should include younger lawyers when they go meet with clients who have asked them to come present on the resources of the firm for a particular piece of business. "We have found that it is terrific for the younger lawyers to watch how the whole process works."

# Chilton Varner

*Chilton Varner has thirty years of courtroom experience as a trial lawyer defending corporations in product liability, business torts, contract, and other commercial disputes. She was identified by the National Law Journal as one of the country's top ten women litigators in December 2001. She is the senior partner in a product liability practice that was selected by Chambers in 2005 and 2006 as one of the top six in the country and by The American Lawyer in January 2004 as one of the top three. The International Who's Who in Product Liability judged her the leading product liability practitioner in Georgia in 2005 and as one of fourteen "most highly regarded" product liability practitioners globally in 2006. She has served as trial and appellate counsel for a number of the country's largest automotive, pharmaceutical and medical device manufacturers. She is experienced in mass tort litigation, class actions and multi-district litigation, including the complex issues of discovery, attorney-client privilege and Daubert challenges to expert testimony that accompany such suits. Ms. Varner was appointed by Chief Justice William Rehnquist in 2004 and re-appointed by Chief Justice John Roberts in 2007 to the Federal Civil Rules Advisory Committee, where she has participated in the Committee's recent drafting of amendments governing electronic discovery and consideration of possible changes to the rules governing summary judgment and expert discovery.*

*Ms. Varner is a native of Opelika, Alabama, a town of 15,000. She joined King & Spalding after receiving her JD, with distinction, Order of the Coif, from Emory University School of Law. She is a Phi Beta Kappa graduate of Smith College in Northampton, Massachusetts. In 1983, she became the second woman partner at King & Spalding and the first woman partner in the Litigation Practice Group. In 1995, she became the first woman elected to the firm's management committee. She has served as a trustee of Emory University since 1995, a director of Wesley Woods Geriatric Center from 1996 to 2007, and a director of the Atlanta Symphony Orchestra since 2005. She is married to K. Morgan Varner, an attorney, and has one daughter, Ashley, who is an oncology social worker at Johns Hopkins Hospital in Baltimore.*

# Paul Webb

Retired Partner
Holland & Knight

Not many people are happy when they lose a hard-fought election. But looking back on his ill-fated campaign for Fulton Superior Court Judge in 1964, Paul Webb Jr. said, "I would have gone absolutely insane if I had to sit on a bench all day and listen to incompetent lawyers arguing cases, which so many of them are. I've been eternally glad that I was not elected and I went on to have a wonderful practice after that."

Even though he lost that election, Mr. Webb said that the process of running for office opened many doors for him in his legal practice and in community service. Other areas that he points to as instrumental in building his practice were the work he did with the Bar, and the United Methodist Church and his involvement with many community organizations such as The Girls Club of Atlanta, the Atlanta Legal Aid Society, Planned Parenthood of Atlanta and similar groups. While none of these efforts was directed to attracting clients, they did introduce him to an enormous group of people, which included many of the progressive business leaders of Atlanta and throughout the country. This in turn contributed to an extremely successful legal career. The firm he founded, Webb & Daniel, merged in 1994 with the international firm of Holland & Knight, from which he retired in 2002.

But building a successful law firm was not Mr. Webb's primary motivation for choosing this career path. It was more altruistic: he simply wanted to leave the world a better place than he found it. His father, Paul Webb Sr., was an ordained Methodist minister. While he never left the ministry, Paul Webb Sr. did give up pastoring and returned to practice law, which he had done before going to Candler School of Theology (now Emory University) when the younger Mr. Webb was just four years old.

"My father felt he could be of better service to the community and to humanity as a lawyer than as a minister," said Mr. Webb. "He convinced me that law was a profession in which I, also, could be of service and strive to leave the world a better place than I found it. That is the reason I went to law school. My father gave me books to read on the lives and the work of great lawyers and from the time I was thirteen or fourteen he would let me go to the courtroom with him when he was trying cases and into peoples' homes when he was interviewing witnesses. From that time on I was dedicated to the law and the possibilities it offered, not for the making of large sums of money, but for service. I felt then as I feel now that my father was the greatest lawyer I ever knew and I thank him for the example and encouragement he gave me."

Mr. Webb, who was born in Macon, Georgia, grew up in Lavonia, Georgia, where he attended school. After high school he attended North Georgia College for two years. It was one of about seven essentially military colleges in the United States from which graduates were commissioned directly into the United States Army. After two years of this intense military training, and in the depth of the Depression, Mr. Webb had to leave college because of lack of funds. He then worked for R.G. LeTourneau Company, an industrial company in Toccoa, Georgia for a year and a half in the machine shop and foundry.

> "I felt then as I feel now that my father was the greatest lawyer I ever knew and I thank him for the example and encouragement he gave me."

Then on December 7, 1941, the entire world as he had known it turned upside down.

"When I was nineteen, the war came along. I had been to military school in Dahlonega and one day my father wanted my mother and me to ride up there for the Sunday parade, a full-dress parade that was a tradition of the school. We drove up on a beautiful December day and watched the parade with the drum major coming down the field, twirling his baton in the air and the band was playing "Stars and Stripes Forever.'

"The battalion behind him was all in step and my spine shivered with tingles as the sun sparkled on the drum major's baton and the flag went by. I suppose that the military tradition lives in my blood. My great-grandfather died in Virginia in the 45th Georgia Regiment, fighting for the Confederacy in 1862. My father ran away and joined the Army in 1917 and fought in France during World War I. Both of my brothers and I did the same during World War II. But back to December 7, 1941 – we went to the Smith House for lunch and then drove home.

"On the way we heard about the Japanese attack on Pearl Harbor. Back home during supper we discussed the situation only briefly. It was agreed with only a little dissension from my mother that the only response for me was to enlist immediately in the defense of America. At that time my father was working in Atlanta as Deputy Head of the Selective Service Board of Georgia. He liked to be at his desk at eight o'clock and to do that he had to leave Lavonia at four o'clock in the morning. We got up a little earlier that morning and I went down to Atlanta with him. He took me to Fort McPherson and dropped me off and an hour later I was in the Army for the duration."

Mr. Webb served in the Field Artillery from December 8, 1941 until September 1946. He graduated from the Artillery Officer Candidate School, Air Force basic flight training school, and the Field Artillery Flight Training School for Liaison Pilots. He served as Liaison Pilot in the 71st Infantry Division in Europe as part of the Third Army, commanded by General George Patton until the surrender of Germany in 1945, and for an additional year in the Occupation Army in Germany until September 1946. He returned to the States and was discharged with the rank of Captain to join the Army Reserve Corps assigned to the 82nd Airborne Division Artillery Headquarters, based in Atlanta.

After returning from Europe, Mr. Webb attended Emory University for five quarters. By doubling up on his courses he completed the academic work necessary for graduation. But it was not enough. Emory required six quarters residence for graduation, which created a problem. Harvard Law School required a college degree for admission.

## "Education for a lawyer isn't just about law. It's also about history, literature, ethics, religion, and morality."

"I argued with Emory without success. Likewise with Harvard. Harvard did admit that I had completed everything necessary for admission, save the formality of graduation, and admitted me for the 1948 class, a year away, but not for 1947. Since I had already lost five years in the war and was twenty-five years old I did not want to wait another year. I enrolled for the 1947 year at the University of Georgia but continued to argue with Harvard. Finally, after the exchange of four or five letters, Harvard relented and let me enter the incoming class of 1947. I went back to Emory during the summer of 1948 and completed the essential quarter for an Emory degree."

Mr. Webb graduated from Harvard Law School in 1950 having taken and passed the Georgia Bar Exam and been admitted to the State Bar in 1949. Although he graduated from a top law school, he doesn't always advise people to go that route.

"Education for a lawyer isn't just about law. It's also about history, literature, ethics, religion, and morality. I've often said that if a person thinking about going into law had the choice between going to a first-class liberal arts college and then to a night school for law school, or turn it around and go to a mediocre liberal arts college and then Harvard, Emory, or some other top-rated law school, he'd be better off to take the first choice. In my opinion, you cannot be a great lawyer without a foundation in the humanities, in history, and especially the moral philosophies."

After graduation Mr. Webb returned to Atlanta, where he interviewed with many established firms for a job, without significant success. "The going rate for beginning associates in Atlanta in 1950 was one hundred dollars per month. Without exception the advice was that, if hired, I need give up any thought of a social life or dating, much less getting married. My time was to be owned by the law firm. Smythe Gambrell, a great lawyer, offered me a job, and said he would pay me two hundred dollars a month, but I'd have to go to his New York office. But he was a friend of mine and advised me not to take it. He said, 'I think one day you'll want to have your own firm, and you won't ever be head of this firm. I have two sons in it and I've got Jim Hill, (who later became a Federal Appellate court judge) all of whom will be ahead of you. I have a place for you if you want it, but I recommend that you go out on your own.'"

So Mr. Webb opened his solo office in small quarters in the office of Bertram Boley, a friend of his father's who had just left a large firm.

"He had a small room in his office for me so I moved in with him. He was a tax lawyer but he had quite a few clients who needed a trial lawyer, and he would turn over to me all the litigation that he had. While I knew virtually nothing about trial practice

*Paul Webb in 1964.*

I managed to avoid any fatal goofs with the help of many experienced lawyers who graciously helped me out, oftentimes when I was on the opposite side of a case. I stayed there with Bertram for eight years. I tried cases all the time and was in the Supreme Court of Georgia within six months of getting out of law school. I made a fair living, married, and started a family. Over the years I received several offers to join large firms, but whenever we sat down and opened our books we found I was earning more than they were paying so I never went with another law firm."

Mr. Webb primarily handled civil cases, although he had a few criminal ones early in his practice. It wasn't by choice – there was simply no way to avoid them.

"In the early days there were no public defenders. If you went to a calendar call for a civil trial, the presiding judge would also have a calendar of criminal cases he had to try. So he would see you sitting out there and he'd point his finger at you and then you'd have a criminal client. I was appointed on quite a few felony cases and burglary cases. I tried three murder cases in my life and quite a few serious personal injury cases, on both sides, sometimes for the plaintiff and sometimes for the defendant. But I could never handle one of those cases involving personal suffering without becoming personally involved with either my client or the suffering client on the other side. It was emotionally draining. I never overcame this problem."

Years later, when Mr. Webb was president of the Atlanta Legal Aid Society, he worked on establishing the first public defender program in Georgia. He traveled all over the Southeast to enlist support for similar programs. At one point he was speaking to the DeKalb County Bar Association in support of the defender program when one of the Superior Court judges stood up and said, "Paul, we don't need a public defender in DeKalb County. We don't indict them if they are not guilty!"

Said Mr. Webb, "Such was the attitude of many of the older members of the profession at the time. However justice demanded that it must be done. And so it was. Such is the greatness of the American people and such is one of the opportunities for service in the profession of law."

In 1958 Mr. Webb formed Sheats, Parker & Webb, a law partnership with Guy Parker and Harold Sheats, Fulton County Attorney. Speaking of Mr. Sheats, Mr. Webb said, "I think he was the greatest lawyer I ever practiced with. He was the perfect example of what I said about education. He was a Phi Beta Kappa at Emory and went to night law school. When it came to philosophy, human nature, common sense, and what was right and what was wrong he could draw on the cumulative knowledge of the ages. So armed we had great success in litigation matters. We knew when to turn down cases when our client was clearly in the wrong; we knew when to settle cases when the outcome did not appear to be favorable, and we knew how to plan and try both the hard ones and the easy ones when we thought our client was right. We had one stretch of four years when we must have tried some forty cases without a loss. He was the greatest lawyer before a jury I've ever seen – the product of night law school but with a magnificent humanities education from Emory."

They practiced together until Mr. Sheats retired in 1970. The firm was reorganized as Webb, Parker and Ferguson. With Mr. Sheats retirement, the Fulton County Attorney's office was open. Several people wanted to take over his county attorney duties, including several large law firms. Mr. Webb was offered the position but he had no desire to move his office to the courthouse. This was worked out with the County Commission so that the county attorney was contracted to the law firm with Mr. Webb and his partners – Bob Young, Harold Daniel, Tom Murphy and John Ferguson – to handle the county legal affairs as a firm and split the salary five ways. They handled these duties for several years, until the decision was made by the county to require the county attorney to return to the courthouse. Mr. Webb still had no desire to move to the courthouse, so his partner Bob Young became the county attorney with Mr. Webb as first associate county attorney, a post he held until 1996.

The firm eventually split up over philosophical differences. Mr. Webb and some of the partners were often working seven-day weeks while others wanted a more easygoing practice. Mr. Webb was also traveling a great deal, taking depositions and conducting trials throughout the Southeast.

"I had to go to New York and left an associate in the office working on a brief I wanted ready for Monday. I got back Saturday afternoon. I went to the office and there was no one there and the brief was not finished," he recalled.

He called the associate who told him that another partner had come into the office and had seen him working. The partner told this associate that they didn't work on Saturdays and he needed to be home with his family. And so he left.

"Although I recognized the necessity for time off for family, and always managed to find such time, I felt deeply that our clients needs came first and if work had to be done on Saturday there was no alternative to being in the office until the work was completed."

> "We never went back to an easygoing law practice. It was often seven days a week, twenty-four hours a day."

The firm reorganized with those who wanted the more easygoing style withdrawing and the new firm becoming Webb & Daniel, led by Mr. Webb and his son-in-law Harold Daniel, who was later to become president of the State Bar of Georgia. "We never went back to an easygoing law practice. It was often seven days a week, twenty-four hours a day. We won some and we lost some. We won more than we lost and had a great time doing it."

When Mr. Webb was asked to run for Superior Court Judge of Fulton County, it was against incumbent Judge Durwood Pye, who was admittedly segregationalist in his philosophy and who many believed to be detrimental to the reputation of the Georgia justice system.

Mr. Webb said he is not a crusader, but he has a firm belief that a feeling of compassion is essential to a real lawyer and to his desire to leave the world a better place.

"There is no room in a system of justice for bias and prejudice based on color or national origin. This was especially true with regard the treatment of African Americans in America and particularly in the South in the sixties. I did not want to live in a community where a black father traveling with his little girl would be unable to find a place to spend the night. I didn't want to live in a state where a father has to explain to his eight-year-old child why he or she could not drink out of the same water fountain used by the white children. There are certain things that are right and certain things that are not right, and the way we treated black people after slavery was ended and right on up through the sixties would break my heart. I set out to do something about it in whatever ways I could."

Mr. Webb also believes in the philosophy of altruism, which he said is the most important concept that has historically distinguished the legal and the medical professions from other ways of earning a living.

"I believe that you have to put the interest of your client, put the interest of the law and justice system, put the interest of the public always in front of your own personal interest if they conflict. This theory is eons old. In the days of the Greeks, it was actually poor form for lawyers to charge a fee for the service that they rendered. However, they learned early on to sew pockets into the back of their robes and they expected their clients to slip money into those pockets. That concept is a part of the profession as I saw it, as is the fact that your client, your practice, and the community always come first. That doesn't mean that you don't have to earn a living to support your family. It means that your interest is on the public first, not the making of large sums of money."

In the 1964 judicial race Mr. Webb was endorsed by *The Atlanta Constitution* for his fairness, temperament and record as a lawyer. He was also endorsed by the vast majority of the leading lawyers in town in a paid political ad, and by leaders in the business and black communities, including William Holmes Borders, Martin Luther King Sr. and Benjamin Mays. Eugene Patterson, editor of *The Atlanta Constitution* wrote of Mr. Webb on Sept. 8, 1964, "A moderate and deliberate man of demonstrated fairness, he can look down from the bench upon all citizens alike without having his actions searched by doubts for signs of favor or disfavor."

> "In the days of the Greeks, it was actually poor form for lawyers to charge a fee for the service that they rendered."

Mr. Webb had enough funds pledged for the campaign and polls favored his election by a two-to-one margin on the final day of qualification to run for this post. However, the astute campaign manager for Judge Pye encouraged Donald Hollowell, a prominent African-American civil rights lawyer, to run, misrepresenting the current Georgia law, which required a majority of votes cast to win a judicial race. The campaign manager convinced Mr. Hollowell that the law had been changed and that he could win with only a plurality vote, which he might obtain if Mr. Webb and Judge Pye split the white vote. The law had indeed been changed as indicated. However, what Judge Pye's campaign did not tell Mr. Hollowell was that it had also been changed back to again require a majority vote in line with all other elections in Georgia.

Editorials in *The Atlanta Constitution* advised voters of that. In the same September

8 editorial Eugene Patterson wrote, "Negro leaders have cautioned Negroes that a vote for Hollowell can be a vote to reelect Pye. They have warned against such a gamble, and urged Negroes instead to combine their strength with white moderates in voting for Webb, as the best way to defeat Pye." But Mr. Hollowell stayed in the race. At that point it seemed there was no way for Mr. Webb to win and his campaign contributions dried up.

But Mr. Webb continued the campaign, funded by himself, his family, and a few close friends. He came in second during the regular election, forcing a runoff with Judge Pye, which he narrowly lost. Judge Pye was reelected.

Even though he lost that election, Mr. Webb believes running the campaign brought him many clients and opened many doors, some of which helped him in another important facet of his career – community service.

A cartoon that ran in The Atlanta Constitution endorsing Paul Webb's election as superior court judge.

Although Mr. Webb did not become involved in service organizations to build his practice, he said the people he met through working with these groups often led to new clients.

He was a founder and first vice president of Planned Parenthood of Atlanta. "My close friends would snicker at me that I didn't get involved in that until after we had five children, but nevertheless, I think we did an awful lot of good trying to promote sex education in schools and trying to provide birth control for the people who already had more children than they could support, particularly in impoverished areas overseas."

Mr. Webb also held offices and did fundraising for the Atlanta Girls Club, which has since merged with the Boys Club. He was a director and later president of the Atlanta Legal Aid Society for years, again out of his sense of compassion.

"The rich people could afford to pay a lawyer and the poor people couldn't. We were trying to establish an adequate program so that everybody, rich or poor, could have legal representation when needed."

He traveled all over the Southeast promoting Atlanta Legal Aid. He also served for several years as chairman of the Disciplinary Board of the State Bar of Georgia and believes being active in the legal community is vital for a lawyer to improve his profession, and, incidentally, it does help to build his practice.

"I never missed a meeting of the State Bar from the time I was admitted to the bar until I quit practicing, and that was over fifty years," Mr. Webb said.

One of the people whose support he won during his campaign was the president of a leading Atlanta bank, who told him if he ever needed any help to ask. So Mr. Webb did.

"We needed some state legislation passed for the Atlanta Girls Club and I wanted to get word to Governor Sanders. I knew Mills Lane, president of the Citizens and Southern National Bank, was close to him, so I called his secretary and asked if I could see him. She said that Mr. Lane didn't have a minute to spare and that he was leaving for Europe the next day, but she would slip a note to him. Then she called back and told me to be there the next morning at seven-fifteen. I went in his office, which didn't have a chair in it. He had a stand-up desk – he never sat down. I was there for about thirty seconds and he stopped me; he said that he understood and agreed with me; that he was going to Europe with Governor Sanders that day and would speak to him. A week later we had what we wanted from the Governor. In many instances the doors opened during that 1964 campaign were helpful in my law practice as well as in community work."

Paul Webb at a Memorial Day house party in 1998 in Coral Gables at the home of his closest friend and partner, the late Chesterfield Smith. Leaders of the bar and judiciary in Florida were there and Mr. Webb represented the bar of Georgia. "It was truly one of the most memorable weekends of my life," he said.

Another area of his life where Mr. Webb devoted much of his time that also helped build his practice was his work with the United Methodist Church. From his start as an initially reluctant Sunday School teacher, (he didn't think he was good enough), he became a lay leader in his local church, then began assuming positions of greater responsibility, including district lay leader, conference lay leader of the North Georgia Conference, chairman of Georgia Area Committee to eliminate racial bias in the Church and to merge the Black and White churches into one unified conference; chancellor of the North Georgia Conference of the Church and a member of the National Council of Finance and Administration and of the National Council of Ecumenical Affairs of The Methodist Church. He was a delegate from the United Methodist Church in the United States to the World Methodist Council and to the National Council of Churches and finally a member of the Judicial Council of the United Methodist Church, the highest position a layman may occupy in that Church.

Mr. Webb also worked on many church committees where he was the only lawyer involved, which sometimes led to new clients. "During my work with the church, I met all kinds of business people, particularly insurance people. One of the great things we did was to negotiate a contract of insurance to cover every United Methodist church in the United States. Some of the best work that we do is in the inner city, and those churches were uninsurable at any price. But we negotiated this contract nationally, so that the company agreed to issue an insurance contract on all properties for the United Methodist churches, both those that were low-risk and those rated as high-risk. And in doing that I got to sit down with the leading underwriters and the leading officers of these various fire and casualty insurance companies all over the country."

While not intended to seek business clients, these contacts frequently led to such results, he said. Although Mr. Webb was quite busy with his legal practice, he devoted a great deal of time to these organizations.

"During the most productive years of my practice, I dedicated about 20 percent of my time to the church business, to the Atlanta Girls business, to the Bar business, or things other than practicing law."

Mr. Webb believes every client he ever had came to him by a referral, either from other lawyers or his clients. He was flattered by what happened in the last jury case he tried. A property damage case was settled while the jury was deliberating. "When the judge announced to the jury that the case had been settled, they all gathered around me and three of them asked for my card. They wanted to come see me. And that is the way the business came. We were fairly successful in our trials and if you were successful, then other clients came."

Mr. Webb feels fortunate that he was able to form long-term relationships with many of his clients. "Although I had one or two stinkers for clients, the vast majority of my long-term clients were amongst my best and most enduring friends. I was a pallbearer at funerals for some and I've been best man at weddings of some. I was godfather to the children of several clients at their christenings and once I traveled to Jerusalem for the bar mitzvah for the son of a beloved client."

Other crucial areas that Mr. Webb stresses are key for young lawyers are continued education, professionalism, and dedication.

"Back when I started and right on up to when I quit practicing, every time there was a course offered in a subject that was within my practice, I would go there, to New York or Washington, or wherever. You can never have enough educational background to feel that you are competent to handle the business as long as there is something else out there that you can learn."

Mr. Webb believes that to be a lawyer one has to consider not only his own standards, but also the standards of everyone else. "He has to work to bring the level of professionalism up and work with the younger lawyers. Reflecting on my own experience and beginning practice virtually on my own, I was very green and barely knew the way to the courthouse. However, I had an easy entry into Atlanta because my father was the district attorney and he knew all the lawyers in town. He was very popular. He won four elections and I could knock on the door of virtually any law office in town and expect a friendly reception. I knew nothing and yet these lawyers would sit there and take the time to answer my questions and tell me various things. Sometimes it was ethical, sometimes it was a legal question, sometimes it was a tactical question, but I found that in my day the lawyers then were willing to sit down and help other lawyers, and especially younger ones."

Mr. Webb believes in absolute dedication to the practice of law. "Law is a jealous

> # Mr. Webb believes every client he ever had came to him by a referral, either from other lawyers or his clients.

*Paul Webb in the Stuart plaid kilt he wore on January 25, 1970 at the Burn's Club dinner when he was president of the club in Atlanta. He is now the oldest and longest member of the club, made up of admirers of the Scottish poet Robert Burns.*

mistress. It takes about twenty-four hours a day. You have to be prepared to give that. Always."

His final advice to young attorneys is to do the very best work they are capable of. "When you are in a large law firm and you do exceptional work, the senior partners are going to take notice of it, and they will give you more and more responsible assignments. They will bring the business in and you'll soon find that even though the senior man may sit next to the client in the courtroom, if you are doing the work, the client is usually going to know it, unless you've got an egregiously selfish and greedy man sitting next to you. If so, he is not a professional and you ought to find somewhere else to go."

In 1994, when Mr. Webb was near retirement, he was offered the chance to merge Webb & Daniel with the firm of Holland & Knight, a large international firm in which two of his law school classmates and the man Mr. Webb considers the greatest lawyer of the twentieth century, Chesterfield Smith, were partners. One of them, John Germany, was his closest friend.

"They selected us to be the first Georgia location for Holland & Knight and I never regretted it. I think it's the greatest law firm in the United States and I thought so then. We worked the merger out and John called me the morning we were supposed to sign the papers. He said, 'Paul, we haven't talked about your compensation.' 'I'm not worried about that. I'm not expecting any compensation, I am retiring,' I said. And he said, 'No, you're not.' And I said, 'I'm seventy-two years old, whatever you want to give me will be more than enough.' He asked then if I was agreeable to receive the same as the other senior partners in the firm. That was the deal we made and I did not know what that amount was until I received my first draw check. I did not need to know. It was enough to be reunited with my old friends and with Chesterfield Smith."

Mr. Webb is particularly pleased with Holland & Knight's dedication to community service. Every lawyer in the firm is required to give many hours a year to such service. One year the firm won the award from the United Way for greatest corporate giving in the United States in competition with America's largest corporations. For several years, it received the American Bar Association award for the best pro bono program in a large law firm in the United States. It has received the governor's award in Georgia, and Florida and the equivalent in Washington, DC for the greatest contribution to public education in the states and in the district.

Mr. Webb's family now has produced four generations of lawyers: his father, himself, two of his children, a son and a daughter, and a granddaughter who recently graduated from Yale Law School and is now clerking for Judge R. Lanier Anderson III of the 11th U.S. Circuit Court of Appeals. He hopes future generations feel as passionate about law as he does.

"I look in the mirror every morning and thank God for letting me be a lawyer."

# Summary

- A good lawyer needs a firm foundation of education in the liberal arts. "In my opinion, you cannot be a good lawyer without a foundation in the humanities, in history, and in particular the moral philosophies."

- The concept of altruism in the most important thing that distinguishes the legal and medical professions from other ways of earning a living. "I believe that you have to put the interest of your client, put the interest of the law and justice system, put the interest of the public always in front of your own personal interest if they conflict."

- Working with community service organizations can lead to introductions to business people who may become clients. "During the most productive years of my practice, I dedicated about 20 percent of my time to the church business, to the Atlanta Club business, to the Bar business, or things other than practicing law.

- Continuing education is crucial to a lawyer. "You can never have enough educational background to feel that you are competent to handle the business as long as there is something else out there that you can learn."

- A lawyer should be concerned about his own standards as well as those of others in the legal profession, and older lawyers should work with younger ones. A lawyer has to work to bring the level of professionalism up and work with the younger lawyers.

- To be a good lawyer requires complete dedication. "Law is a jealous mistress. It takes about twenty-four hours a day. You have to be prepared to give that."

# Paul Webb

*Paul Webb Jr. was born in Macon, Georgia. He enlisted in the Army the day after Pearl Harbor and served in the Field Artillery from 1942 to 1946 as a liaison airplane pilot in the field artillery. After attending Emory University, he went to Harvard Law School and graduated in 1950.*

*He returned to the South and started his own firm, which eventually became Webb & Daniel. That firm merged with Holland & Knight in 1994. Mr. Webb served in several positions in the United Methodist Church, including Conference lay leader of the North Georgia Conference, chancellor of the North Georgia Conference and as a member of the General Council of Finance and Administration, the General Council of Ecumenical Council of the United Methodist Church.*

*Mr. Webb served as Fulton County Attorney and as Associate County Attorney from 1971 to 1995. He is a fellow in the American College of Trial Lawyers. He is a member of the Atlanta and American Bar Associations; State Bar of Georgia (Chairman, State Disciplinary Board, 1976, 1977) and Lawyers Club of Atlanta. He is a past president of the Atlanta Legal Aid Society and past chairman of the Disciplinary Board of the State Bar of Georgia. Mr. Webb retired in 2002 at the age of eighty. He now makes his home in Helen, Georgia with his wife, Gwyneth.*

# Addendum

Miles Alexander generously gave his permission to run the following articles that he wrote. The first one he co-wrote with Lisa Pearson, a partner in the New York office of Kilpatrick Stockton. Entitled "Keeping Existing Clients Happy," it first appeared in the *New York Law Journal,* and is reprinted with permission.

# Keep Existing Clients Happy

By Miles Alexander and Lisa Pearson

Satisfied clients can be your staunchest advocates and best source of new work and referrals, so ensure that yours are well served and happy; it's far easier to lose clients than to get new ones.

As a new partner, one of the most important things you can do is to ensure that your existing clients are well served and happy. As you have no doubt learned by now, performing great work alone is just not enough. It is far easier to lose clients than to get new ones. Satisfied clients can be your staunchest advocates and your best source of new work and referrals.

Never forget that law is a service profession. Consider the professionals who serve you: your doctors, your accountant, the lawyer who handled your real estate closing or drafted your will. The professionals you stick with and recommend to others are typically those with whom you have a high comfort level. They understand you. They help you identify your problem, your objectives, and the best solutions. They take good care of you.

Identify the things that create the bond between you and your preferred service providers. Then see if you can adapt them in serving your own clients.

This article lays out five proven ways to keep and develop existing clients, and some practical pointers for implementing them. If they sound like common sense, that's because they are building relationships that lead to new sources of work. Your goal should not just be to serve your clients well, but to deepen and expand your professional relationships.

## 1. Communicate Effectively

Good communication leads to healthy relationships, professional as well as personal.

**Listen.** Professionals are programmed to have the answers, but we can usually come up with much better answers if we pause long enough to listen first. The most basic communication skill is asking good questions that draw out your client's needs and concerns and listening hard to the responses. Beware of hearing what you want to hear.

You can avoid pitfalls if you just take the time at the outset to ask your clients a few simple questions about the scope and importance of the work and discuss the steps necessary to deliver what they want in the format that would be most useful.

**Be Responsive.** Responsiveness demonstrates you care and that your client's problems are important to you. in your absence.

**Provide Regular Updates.** You should endeavor to keep your client fully informed, to educate it as needed on the legal issues (and to educate yourself on the business issues), and to work together as a team to achieve your client's goals.

To this end, get in the habit of confirming the issues presented by your client, as well as your advice, in writing and in plain English. Written confirmation helps you hone your analysis and clarify or expand your oral advice.

Provide regular updates on long-term engagements, particularly with respect to significant changes in cost estimates, since your failure to do so can undermine your client's budget and confidence in you. Do not wait until your client calls you. It is part of your job to keep your client informed of your progress, or explain why there is none.

**Follow Up.** Keep your matters moving by following up on open items within a reasonable period of time, well before your client raises any questions. Use a reliable suspense system that prompts you along the way. Staying on top of things and anticipating deadlines shows your conscientiousness and reliability. It may also spare your client the pain of a last-minute fire drill.

Frequently, you can establish a time-frame for follow-up in your initial communication. For example, when transmitting your comments on the other side's counterproposal on an agreement, you might say: "I would like to reply to opposing counsel by next Wednesday. If I have not heard from you, I will call you on Tuesday to ensure that I have your input."

Of course, following up can do far more than just keeping your matters on track. When you are involved with clients on particular matters, you have a natural reason to stay in touch. How did a planned meeting go? How did your advice work out? Were the business people satisfied with the result? Following up keeps channels of communication open. It is a simple way to reach out to your clients, reaffirming your continuing interest, concern and appreciation for their business.

**Outline Options but Make Recommendations.** Start from the premise that your clients are intelligent people who want to know both their options and your recommendations.

Once you have an established relationship with a client, you will no doubt gain a better understanding of its preferred way of communicating with you and how much detail is necessary. As a general rule, most clients appreciate a straightforward summary of their options, the pros and cons of each, a cost benefit analysis, and the approach you recommend. Conversely, most clients have little need for a lawyer who just passes along information without providing any guidance.

## 2. Add Value

**Never Act as a Mere Conduit.** Whenever you are working on a particular matter, be on the lookout for ways to add value to your client. When you merely act as a conduit – for example, forwarding a set of interrogatories or a draft of an agreement without explanatory comments-you lose a chance to prove your worth.

**Brainstorm and Troubleshoot.** If you are communicating with your client effectively, you are educating it and managing its expectations. You are also learning about its global needs and priorities. You are therefore in a unique position to brainstorm with your client and colleagues about creative solutions to the issues at hand, and to troubleshoot problems that have not yet arisen.

**Bill Fairly.** Too often, lawyers feel they must bill for every minute in their day. This puts them at odds with their clients, almost all of which are cost conscious. No one wants to spend more than the potential exposure warrants. You will earn considerable client loyalty if you are cost-effective, staff matters appropriately, and bill fairly for the work performed.

One useful approach is to review your own time entries, staffing and bills as though another law firm prepared them and your client has asked you whether they are fair and reasonable. often, you may want to add a better explanation of the work performed and results achieved. Sometimes, you may want to reduce fees that appear excessive or give the client a courtesy discount before presenting your bill.

Entire articles have been written on using your bills as a business development tool. If as a new partner you are billing clients for the first time, you may glean some helpful ideas from reading the literature and talking to lawyers and clients about best billing practices. Clearly, you should know your clients' billing expectations, concerns and pet peeves.

## 3. Solve Legal Problems Creatively

**Do Your Research.** You need not limit your research to learning about the other side's principals, counsel, history and prior litigation. Research your own clients to know more about them too. The more you know about the client's business and industry, the better your ability to anticipate, trouble shoot and solve legal problems.

**Identify True Needs and Objectives.** Assuming you are communicating with your client and doing your research, you can help the client identify true needs and objectives and prioritize desired outcomes. This permits you to give pragmatic advice and to keep your eye on the prize.

For example, few clients relish litigation, which is just one solution to a business problem and oftentimes not the best one. Litigators who listen to and hear their clients can often help them achieve their business goals – as well as save time and money – through settlement negotiations, mediation or arbitration at an early stage in the dispute. Keep a checklist of alternative settlement approaches from other cases. Review them with your client to see if any apply and to prompt other ideas.

**Understand the Bigger Picture.** Take as a given that the legal file you have on your desk tells just part of the story. You can be a better problem solver if you spend some time learning the history of the matter, sizing up the importance of the issue, putting yourself in your adversary's shoes, and making ongoing assessments of the available alternatives. Placing the problem in perspective can suggest new solutions and strategies to achieve them.

**Get a Little Help From Your Friends.** In this day and age of ever increasing legal specialization, nobody knows it all. Don't be afraid to bounce your ideas off colleagues or to tap into their expertise. Could an international arbitration clause in your deal document save your client a lot of headaches litigating in a foreign land in the event of a breach? Are there ways to structure a litigation settlement that could minimize tax liability? Are there commercial claims as well as trademark infringement claims arising out of a terminated distribution agreement? In law school we were taught to spot issues. It is one legal skill that has real practical application as you try to solve real problems.

**Think Outside the Box.** U.S. law evolves. It is not carved in stone. Fact patterns differ. And there is generally more than one viable approach to any legal problem. As a result, you can do your clients a favor by questioning conventional wisdom and taking a fresh look at the situation. Few things impress a client more than your ability to offer an elegant solution that hasn't occurred to anyone else before.

## 4. Personalize the Relationship

**Care About Your Clients.** Presumably, you like being a lawyer if you have stayed in the field and jumped over the hurdles to partnership. If your client's issues and concerns (as well as their lives and aspirations) don't interest you, then perhaps you should concentrate on different clients or a different specialty. The best attorney-client relationships grow out of genuine interest, concern and empathy. You cannot feign it.

**Visit Your Client's Workplace.** Nine times out of 10, when you take the time to visit your clients at their places of work, you learn something new. You meet new people; you see new advertising, or packaging, or literature; you hear about new business plans; you find out more about the culture of the client's organization and how it runs and is run.

People are usually more comfortable and candid in their own place of business. It is surprising how often a relatively simple fact you pick up from a client visit provides the key to unlocking a tough legal problem. It is also surprising how often you walk away from a client's workplace with more work in hand.

**Find Your Natural Constituency.** Strive to find your natural constituency – the clients to whom you can relate. Then the rest will flow naturally. At this stage in your career, you may not be interacting with top business and legal officers. Still, your client contacts may influence legal hiring decisions, and they may well feel more comfortable working on a daily basis with you than a senior partner with whom they have little in common. In due course, your in-house peers will be promoted or move to other positions elsewhere. Someday, if it is not happening already, your contemporaries are going to be heading up legal departments and companies, and sitting on the bench, and running for President. Get to know them now and you increase your access and credibility later.

**Try to Understand 'Difficult' Clients.** Clients, like everyone else, have idiosyncrasies. make allowances. Be patient. Sometimes, you may need to tell a client, gently but firmly, what you need and expect in order to do your best for it. In law as in life, there are good and bad matches. Try to make a better match if you are not the right lawyer for the client. If you just can't make it work after giving it your best shot, focus your energy on better prospects.

**Be Generous and Helpful.** Clients may or may not be personal friends. But building solid friendships and building solid business relationships have much in common. Put aside the notion that each of your business development activities should immediately translate into more business. It doesn't usually work that way. Instead, cast your bread upon the water.

Be generous and helpful where you can. Introduce people in your network who may be useful to each other. offer your ear and support to clients going through big changes or tough periods. Be thoughtful. Provide updates on legal developments of interest without charge. most likely, your kindnesses will be repaid in ways you can't even predict.

**Celebrate Successes.** What better way to bond with a client than over an achievement or success? Celebrate successes every chance you get. Remember to compliment the good work of others, both within your organization and within your client's. Give credit where credit is due. It reflects well on you, as well as the subject of your praise, and will be remembered.

**Socialize.** Let's face it. Some people genuinely enjoy business entertainment while others view it as a chore. Certainly, meeting with clients outside of the work environment can help you find common ground, understand each other better and work together more effectively. It personalizes the relationship, and makes doing business more fun. Try to find or create social events that you and your clients will both enjoy. Very few people will be put off by a thoughtful invitation.

## 5. Invest for the Future

**Invest in Your Existing Clients.** If you have ever prepared a response to an RFP or competed in a beauty contest, you know how many non-billable hours go into chasing a new potential client. Chances are that if you invest a fraction of that time in providing better service to an existing client, you will reap the reward in more work from that client and a stronger relationship in the future. So go the extra yard, even if you can't bill for it.

**Read Industry Publications.** One easy way to stay ahead of the curve is to read industry publications and news stories of interest to your client. Sending along clippings with a personal note is a great way to show you are thinking about your client.

**Provide Ideas and Strategies Without Charge.** Think again about how much non-billable time you would be willing to spend to bring in a substantial new piece of work or a viable new client, even if you were not the leading contender for the work. Now consider: Would it make sense to redirect some of that non-billable time to providing some ideas, strategies and other work product to long-time clients who know and appreciate you? Just because a client is already in the door does not mean you need to bill for every jot and title. Offering something of value (your time) at no charge is one way you can be helpful and generous without spending a cent.

**Integrate Other Lawyers Into the Relationship.** Most enlightened firms value teamwork. They reward partners for expanding client relationships and broadening the scope of work. From an institutional point of view, law firm stability comes from having a team of lawyers working together to serve the best interests of clients.

For most people, cross-selling others within their firm is far easier than self-promotion. Clients sometimes don't know that their preferred firm has sufficient depth and bench strength to handle more transactions or cases than they have already entrusted to the firm. Bringing colleagues into the mix often leads to more sophisticated advice, and it allows more personal relationships to develop at different levels of the client organization.

For all of these reasons, we strongly advocate integrating other lawyers into the client relationship when the appropriate opportunity presents itself. That said, you need to be sensitive to areas in which the client already has outstanding counsel, particularly where those lawyers have brought you into the picture, and treat them as you would have other counsel treat you.

**Ask for Feedback.** Your firm may or may not have formal client satisfaction surveys. Regardless, that should not stop you from conducting informal surveys yourself. Borrow mayor Ed Koch's line: "How are we doing?"

Then follow up: "How can we improve? Do you have any issues or concerns with our work product? The lawyers you worked with? Your bills?" It never hurts to tell a favorite client that you value the relationship. Don't take good clients for granted.

**Act on Feedback.** Of course, once you've asked for feedback, act on it promptly. See how you can best address any points on which your client believes there is room for improvement, and then check in on your progress. Small aggravations have a way of festering. Identify them early and eradicate them.

## In Conclusion

We firmly believe that successful business development plans flow from maintaining and developing existing client relationships proactively and as a matter of course. No doubt, you are already employing many of the tips summarized above, consciously or unconsciously. If not, give them a try. They work.

*Miles Alexander and Lisa Pearson are intellectual property partners in Kilpatrick Stockton, Mr. Alexander in its Atlanta office and Ms. Pearson in New York. Mr. Alexander is also co-chair of the firm.*

# Tender Loving Care of Clients

By Miles Alexander

### 1. You have to really care!

The client knows real as opposed to the appearance of empathy. No matter how simple or complex, real or unreal the problem, you must address it seriously and with sincere concern about reaching a reasonable solution.

### 2. Responsiveness.

A call must be promptly returned, and meetings immediately scheduled if necessary. Lawyers who let their phone messages pile up to be returned late in the day, or at the lawyer's convenience, will often find clients looking elsewhere for assistance. The same is true when one of your law partners or associates call, for if you leave them waiting it often impacts firm's clients for whom they have primary responsibility. If you're in court or on a trip, call in on your breaks. Make certain you have your secretary or another lawyer return the call to advise the client of your unavailability and to see if someone else can help. Call back at lunch or to their home at night to see if the matter is critical. Your concern about responding is meaningful to the client – just as when a doctor returns your call promptly, or calls to see how the treatment is working, is evidence of the fact that they care and are responsive. One without the other is not enough.

### 3. Confirm your advice in writing – even if it is only sending a copy of your memo to the file.

Often putting something in writing will serve several purposes: (i) it will help you deal with a related problem for that client in the future when you pick up the file a year or more later; (ii) if you are unavailable for follow-up advice or when the problem arises again, it is an immense help to your colleague who picks up the file, both as to the substance and style and form of the advice given to that client, and in educating your colleague about the client; (iii) it provides confirmation about the advice given to the client, which studies indicate is often forgotten by the client – not merely for the purpose of protecting you and your firm, but in order to emphasize the importance of a warning you have given a client about what not to do, as well as what to do, and to give the client a chance to digest the advice; (iv) it often helps the client understand a statement for legal services, where a phone call might not make apparent the substantive considerations involved in the advice; (v) I often find that in reducing my opinions to writing it raises other considerations that should have been dealt with in the phone call, and it permits elaboration and supplemental relevant advice – often even the form of a suggested letter or contract provision, etc.

### 4. Follow-up!

Do you recall receiving a call from your doctor after taking medication for a fever or some other illness following a visit to his or her office, or following surgery? How impressive that they cared and took time to see how you were doing and whether your problem was solved. Too few lawyers take the time to determine how a meeting went, or the effectiveness of the advice given. Most clients are impressed by follow-up calls – particularly at home if the day does not permit – or from out of town. Fifteen minutes a day on the phone from out of town or out of the country on vacation need not ruin your trip and can provide both you and your clients with peace of mind.

## 5. Use a suspense system.

Bringing matters to the attention of clients before they realize follow-up action is required demonstrates your thoroughness and reliability. It also permits advance consideration of decisions that need to be made on a non-crisis basis. Whether a contract or lease renewal, a change in the law requiring re-examination of agreements, or a routine scheduled government filing, the reminder from an attorney justifiably leaves a favorable impression with most clients. A personal calendar, computer or hard copy office suspense system, or a combination is helpful. I often place an extra copy of a relevant letter, memo, or document in suspense for the future – whether it be for thirty days or five years later. Before leaving on vacation, it is often helpful to review these suspense files to see what may become due while you are gone. It is also helpful to remind others in your firm to follow up on matters involving you and another lawyer.

## 6. Advise clients regularly of changes in the law.

Whether it is time for your clients to review their wills or consider the impact of a new trade secret law, it is better they hear about it from their lawyer, rather than in the newspaper, or through an accountant, insurance agent or others. Don't be merely a reactive lawyer – real counseling requires the proactive practice of law.

## 7. Give credit where credit is due.

Too many lawyers are slow to acknowledge the contribution of their colleagues to solving a client's problem. We should bask in the glow of having able lawyers and paralegals and staff in our office who contribute to the quality of services rendered. It provides the client with a justifiable sense of confidence in dealing with your firm. Where justified, promote the bright young lawyer or peer colleague to the client. You gain for yourself and your firm justifiable client confidence in your good judgment in selecting the right lawyer to help them. Similarly, do not blame someone else for your own oversight.

## 8. Recognize your client's idiosyncrasies and adjust.

Some clients are unreasonably demanding while others reluctant "to bother" you. Make allowances for those differences. You cannot treat all clients as fungible. Match the right lawyer with the right clients – do not try to mix oil and water. A short-tempered or impatient lawyer rarely can help an unreasonable, slow-to-grasp, or stubborn client. A lawyer whose own temperament does not deal well with pressure or is short with clients often is very able, but is subject to having their services limited to legal work without client contact.

## 9. Be a person as well as a lawyer.

Some clients look at their lawyers as "hired guns" and have no interest in extending contact outside working hours. Others are too busy to socialize except in the context of a working luncheon or trip. However, others feel it is important for their lawyers to know them and their families in human dimensions – and it is important that you recognize this desire and need. Many clients' legal problems will have a serious impact on their own lives, as well as on that of their families. They reasonably require emotional as well as legal support. Indeed, it is not infrequent or inappropriate to have some of your clients become your good friends.

## 10. Professionalism.

Treat your opponents and their lawyers with courtesy and respect. Every battle need not be a holocaust. Litigation, negotiations, and other adversarial relationships should not be unnecessarily confrontational, and should never be personalized in terms of allegations of bad faith, disingenuousness, insecurity, etc. One can be firm without being abrasive. Civility is not a sign of weakness. Always have your client pretend that he or she is on the opposite side in order to better understand their own position as well as their opponents, and to better understand the range of amicable solutions available. Your reputation among your fellow lawyers will often help or haunt you with your clients. Unnecessarily embarrassing your adversary seldom yields the best results for one's clients.

## 11. Do not be the type of lawyer who is part of the problem rather than part of the solution.

Nothing can more justifiably undermine client confidence than unnecessary and costly discovery battles, procedural battles, unreasonable negotiation positions, and an absence of creative problem solving by counsel.

## 12. Cost consciousness.

Bills for legal services should be drafted and reviewed as if you were the client reviewing it for reasonableness. Pretend that the bill was being sent by another firm to your client and you had been asked to review it for reasonableness. Remember: law practice is not merely a business; it is a profession. Time devoted to the matter is one of many factors that may help to determine the reasonableness of a bill for services rendered. It is not an inflexible measure of the value of legal services. Unproductive time may actually have created rather than solved a problem. When asking an associate to research an issue, provide guidance as to how extensive you expect that research to be before he or she reports back. Every question does not require a lengthy research memorandum, and when one is desirable for your own security in rendering advice, it is not necessarily billable. Clients should not be expected to pay for law review articles. On the other hand, a carefully crafted, lengthy opinion letter for another client on a similar matter may make your five-minute telephone advice far more valuable to the client than that which would be reflected in a statement measured only by time. Similarly, whether the proposed transaction is consummated, financial problems of the client and the startup nature of the business are just a few of the many factors that should be considered in drafting a bill. Some of a lawyer's best and most loyal clients are often those who were billed little or nothing at their embryonic stages of development.

## 13. Put yourself in the place of your clients when you consider fees.

You know your reaction when you receive a dry cleaning bill, a plumbing bill, a doctor's bill or a dentist bill that is unusually high. Give your client the same courtesy of recognizing their reactions to your bills as you would have in their place. Time records and budget fees are merely a guide to assist you in billing, although in many and perhaps most instances they might reflect a reasonable basis for charges to the client. In many instances, as everyone knows, they reflect learning time, excessive personnel dealing with the matter for the firm's own convenience, or excessive research on a matter that did not require an in-depth memorandum or research. Always ask yourself, if you were the client would you have a reasonable basis for resenting the fee? Sensitivity to that question and to even such apparently minor matters as reviewing the disbursements charged to a client on the bill will often preserve a relationship.

## 15. Educate your clients.

Most of us represent very intelligent people. They should not be treated as many doctors treat their patients, i.e., just do as I say, there is no need for you to understand the problem, I'm the doctor. A client knows their business better than anyone else, and if the legal principles are explained to them, they can often creatively contribute to solving the problem at hand – become part of a team effort dedicated to that goal – and appreciative of the opportunity to do so.

## 16. Keep the client informed of your progress, or why there is none.

Delays by government agencies, opposing counsel or the courts should not be something that you assume clients expect. A non-response to a demand letter should be suspensed so you can write to the client to say that we still have not heard and to propose a course of action. Do not wait until the client calls to ask, "Whatever happened on the matter involving…."

## 17. Provide the client with cost estimates for activities that are likely to involve significant or unexpected legal fees and/or disbursements.

Do not let bills accumulate. Where possible for a client to choose between different cost alternatives, provide information on those alternatives and give the client an intelligent basis for making a choice.

## 18. Provide the client with a realistic analysis of the likelihood of success in negotiations, litigation, or other transactions, as well as cost factors.

Do not be overly aggressive in feeding a client's sense of self-righteousness. Nor should you be a naysayer, only wringing your hands and pointing out the negatives. Make it clear that a thirty percent chance of losing means three out of every ten cases.

## 19. Simplify where possible.

(Executive Summary) The client can't always expect a yes or no answer, but nor should the client have to deal with all of the lawyer's insecurities about rendering advice. Give your conclusions succinctly and, where many caveats are required, provide the client with the succinct recommendation or conclusion and then the lengthier discussion.

## 20. Don't fake it.

No one knows all the answers and nothing causes a loss of confidence faster than a wrong answer off the top of your head. Do not hesitate to say, "I don't know, but I'll quickly find out."

## 21. Treat every firm client as you would your personal client.

All clients are entitled to, and appreciate receiving the same conscientious attention, whether or not the lawyer whom they normally call upon is available.

## 22. Keep your colleagues informed.

If you know the client may be dealing with another lawyer in the firm in your absence, or if the primary client contact is another lawyer, keep that colleague copied or informed. It is embarrassing when clients ask about their case or problem and a lawyer closest to the client who should know the status does not have a clue.

## 23. Confidentiality.

The confidences in your client's affairs are sacred. If you talk about other client's matters, whether or not confidential, the clients to whom you make those comments know that their affairs are similarly being shared with others and, consciously or subconsciously, you've lost some degree of their respect. Similarly, sensitive personal matters about clients are not meant to be shared within the office, except where necessary. A client does not assume that by sharing a confidence with you he or she is authorizing you to share it with your colleagues.

## 24. Treat everyone with courtesy and respect no matter what their level of responsibility.

The person you are dealing with may head the client in ten years. Few things are resented more by people than being treated as non-entities, too insignificant for your attention and the common courtesy that everyone deserves. More important, lawyers who select those people who they think are important to them and ignore those remaining will invariably live to regret their shortsightedness. Just like most lawyers have risen from "lowly freshmen," "first-year law students" and "beginning associates," so many lower echelon employees and clients will rise. Whether the person is a parking lot attendant, a sales person, a junior executive, a secretary or an assistant to an assistant, you will feel better and that person will feel better if you treat them with respect and interest. You will not only broaden your own horizons and make friends, but those giving your clients a boost and yourself a boost in future years will frequently come from the group that you least expect it to assist you. It is not enough that this attitude merely be reflected around courthouse clerical people who most lawyers realize are in a position to cause them untold misery if offended. One interesting example of the same situation is the case of a lawyer who many years ago offended a receptionist at the firm when he was a young associate. So one day he decided to go to a noon movie instead of lunch. He left his umbrella at the movie and when the umbrella was returned, the receptionist announced it over the loud speaker. All the senior partners of the firm were in the library, and chuckled. People who know you are a nice person and can only judge it by the way you treat them will go out of their way to help and protect you. Those who are given another impression even if erroneously will often go out of their way to harm you and will look for the opportunity to do so.

## 25. Relationship with other lawyers.

Your relationship with other lawyers outside the firm will often be critical to your obtaining a client and obtaining good results for existing clients. When considering the selection of an attorney, many business people speak to lawyers they know to ascertain your reputation. Thus, your general demeanor with other lawyers, as well as your Bar Association activities and competence, all go into your image and reputation.

Whether dealing with an older lawyer, a younger lawyer, or someone outside your field, your courtesy to them and your comments about them, as well as your reputation in terms of competence and integrity, all go into the formula of what is said about you. Similarly, you should make your comments about other lawyers with the same good judgment of trying to speak well of everyone unless there is an overriding reason not to do so. A pejorative reference in a brief is not only counterproductive with the Court, but can make settlement of your client's case more difficult and expensive.

## 26. Settlement and ADR.

One of the more difficult problems in dealing with clients is the desire that most have to feel that their lawyer is aggressively advocating their position and taking a very positive approach about the righteousness of that position. Unfortunately, the cost of sustaining one's position is frequently far beyond the value of what a successful result would obtain for the client. Although this concept and many others are axiomatic to the practice of law and merely good common sense, the failure of a lawyer to discuss amicable resolution of problems at a minimal cost at the very initial stages of a dispute can endanger the long-term relationship with the client when excessive costs are incurred over a period of time. The client may look back at the whole matter in retrospect and decide that full advice was not given early enough about the potential consequences of the dispute.

# Acknowledgements

"Commitment is a line you must cross...it is the difference between dreaming and doing."
– *Bernie Fuchs*

I was reminded of this quote when people would ask me how I continued to see forty clients a week and still pull this book together. Although this book has definitely been a challenge on many levels, it is the fulfillment of a dream for me, and the commitment to the time, resources and effort it took has been worth it all.

I am surrounded by the inspiration for creating this book and DVD: my clients. As a coach of some of the best and brightest of their profession, I help some of the smartest, top-notch professionals find greater success in a field they love. However, most do not have that same passion for marketing. They constantly amaze me with their determination and dedication to their clients, their firms and business development. And I feel fortunate that many of my clients are my friends as well. I have the greatest job in the world and am proud to say that it is one I created myself.

I was also inspired to create this book and DVD so I could help support an organization I am passionate about – the Atlanta Legal Aid Society. I am in awe of the work they do every day to help those in need.

Many of the attorneys I interviewed for this book talk about the need to give credit and to compliment your partners. Judge Bell tells of Hughes Spalding bragging on everyone in the King & Spalding law firm. Well, now it's my turn to credit my partners in this project.

First, I must thank all ten people who agreed to participate in this book and shared generously both of their time and their wisdom. I have so much admiration and respect for these amazingly talented and accomplished people. It is one of my greatest honors that they each agreed to be a part of this project and I was able to commemorate and preserve the advice of these dynamic leaders. Thank you to Miles Alexander, Judge Bell, Emmet Bondurant, Bobby Lee Cook, Clay Long, Frank Love, Carl Sanders, Richard Sinkfield, Chilton Varner, and Paul Webb.

The book and DVD also would not have been possible without the people at Schroder Public Relations, my publishers. Their team took on this project as their own and has helped me realize my vision of what I wanted it to be. Jan Butsch Schroder is my writer and editorial director and guided me through the unfamiliar world of publishing. Reid Childers is the producer and director of all the videos. Chris Schroder is my publisher and provided much guidance as well, and Evelyn Anne Johnston helped as a videographer's assistant and with obtaining photographs.

Thanks go to Dave Poston of Poston Communications, who is spearheading my marketing efforts. As Judge Bell said, "If you've got a good product, why not tell people about it?"

I wish to thank those who helped me acquire the cooperation of our distinguished group of interviewees. In particular, they are Sidney Kirschner, Jill Pryor, Josh Thorpe, Laurie Webb Daniel, and all the people at King & Spalding who helped us communicate with Judge Bell. And many thanks to all the attorneys' assistants and other members of their law firms who facilitated the process. Judge Dorothy Beasley offered me endless wise advice during the selection process.

I want to thank all of you who help me "raise the bar" every day. John Teichert, my best friend and partner; Jill Pryor, whose friendship and consultation are priceless; my dear friend Beverly Molander, whose contribution to this book and to my life is invaluable; and Sidney Kirschner, who is the greatest mentor, advisor, and friend anyone could ask for. Thanks go to the staff and volunteers of the Atlanta Legal Aid Society, especially Executive Director Steve Gottlieb, Director of Communications and Annual Giving Angie Tacker and Paula Lawton Bevington, former Atlanta Legal Aid Board President and present head of the endowment campaign. Thank you to Bill Johnson, who nominated me to the Atlanta Legal Aid Society advisory board in 2004 to take his place.

And thanks to the many others, too numerous to mention, who have touched my life in positive ways.

Here's to Raising the Bar.


*Robin M. Hensley*

# Index

# Robin M. Hensley

Robin M. Hensley has built a legacy of success in the business community. She now serves as a business development coach, assisting individuals in achieving their professional goals and objectives. She specializes in coaching attorneys and CPAs who are at the top of their game, in order to maximize their rainmaking skills. Her record of involvement in numerous community organizations demonstrates Robin's strong commitment to people and their development.

Robin served on the board of directors of Northside Hospital. She also serves on the board of directors of Superior Uniform Group, listed on NASDAQ, where she chairs the audit committee.

An honors graduate in accounting from Georgia State University, Robin received the Georgia State University School of Accounting's Distinguished Alumnus award. She was with Ernst & Young for five years and the Atlanta law firms of Kilpatrick Stockton and Swift, Currie, McGhee & Hiers in both marketing and business development roles for more than six years.

Her honors include Atlanta Legal Aid Society advisory board of directors, Leadership Atlanta alumnae, honorary lifetime member of the board of the American Cancer Society, *Business Atlanta Magazine's* "Top 40 under 40," and *Atlanta Business Chronicle's* "Top 20 Self-made Women of Atlanta." Robin's work as a business development coach has been featured in numerous publications including the *Atlanta Business Chronicle* and *Atlanta Journal-Constitution*. She is the exclusive executive coach for Atlanta's *Business to Business* magazine. She can be reached at rhensley@raisingthebar.com